Your Words
Hold *a* Miracle

WITH COMMENTARY AND A FOREWORD BY

Joel Osteen

Your Words
Hold *a* Miracle

THE POWER OF SPEAKING GOD'S WORD

JOHN OSTEEN

New York | Boston | Nashville

Literary development and design: Koechel Peterson & Associates, Inc., Minneapolis, Minnesota.

FaithWords
Hachette Book Group
237 Park Avenue, New York, NY 10017
www.faithwords.com.

The publisher is not responsible for websites (or their content) that are not owned by the publisher.

FaithWords is a division of Hachette Book Group, Inc.

Printed in the United States of America.

First Printing: May 2012

10 9 8 7 6 5 4 3 2 1
ISBN: 978-0-892-96882-4

Library of Congress Control Number: 20129316 78

CONTENTS

DEDICATION

I wish my heart could say in words the love and respect I have for the man John Osteen. The love of my life, my pastor, the father of my children, and a gentle person, full of love, mercy, and compassion. Married for forty-four years, four months, and six days was way too short. The fact is, now we are separated, him in a mansion and me in my earthly home, but someday we'll live in eternity together.

My husband taught me faith, and how to believe God and receive a miracle, which I did in 1981 when diagnosed with metastatic cancer of the liver and given a few weeks to live. That was thirty years ago, and soon I will be seventy-eight. More than a few weeks, don't you think? I am alive today because of the teachings of great men of God, and one of them was my husband. He always said, "Store up the Word of God in your heart when you don't need it, and you will have it when you do need it."

It is so important what words come out of our mouth. I encourage you to read the Word of God, heed what it teaches, be obedient to God's commandments, and remind God of His Word. As you do this, God's Word will come alive in your heart, and you will see signs, wonders, and miracles in your life and the lives of others whom you touch.

Thank God, Jesus never changes.

DODIE OSTEEN

FOREWORD BY JOEL OSTEEN

IF YOU'VE BEEN A PART OF OR WATCHED one of our services at Lakewood Church, you know that at the beginning of each service, I have everyone hold up their Bible and repeat after me,

This is my Bible.
I am what it says I am.
I have what it says I have.
I can do what it says I can do.
Today, I will be taught the Word of God.
I boldly confess my mind is alert.
My heart is receptive.
I will never be the same.
I am about to receive the incorruptible,
*   indestructible, ever-living seed*
*   of the Word of God.*
I will never be the same. Never, never, never!
I will never be the same.

IN JESUS' NAME. AMEN.

It might surprise you to discover that my father incorporated the use of this marvelous statement of faith into our services long before I began to pastor the church. This confession of the central role of the Word of God in believers' lives was the driving force in his life, and he never allowed our family or our congregation to forget it. Regarding everything that relates to our lives, my dad would always remind us of what "the Bible says."

Daddy came to know the power of declaring the Word of God and was so adamant about teaching it because he grew up in an environment where most people, if they were being honest, would say, "I don't have what the Bible says I can have, and I am not doing what it says I can do. I just remain the same, the same, the same." Many of them didn't know what God has stated in His Word, and few believed we are what the Bible says we are.

I've discovered the same to be true today, which is why I continue this declaration in our services. The Bible is filled with powerful statements about who we are in Christ and what belongs to us as believers. Some of the statements are so amazing that when we read them, I

IF YOU WANT TO CHANGE

YOUR WORLD,

start by changing your words

to those taken straight from

the Word of God.

think we don't really hear them in our spirit. The promises are so grand that even when we do see them, it just doesn't compute. The natural mind is so far removed from the reality of our spirit that the truth doesn't feel real to us.

As you'll soon discover in this book, if you want to change your world, start by changing your words to those taken straight from the Word of God. When you're facing obstacles in your path, you must learn to boldly say, "Greater is He who is in me than he who is in the world" (see 1 John 4:4); "No weapon formed against me is going to prosper" (see Isaiah 54:17); and "God always leads me to triumph" (see 2 Corinthians 2:14).

My dad would tell people that rather than complaining about poverty or lack they should start declaring, "God supplies all of my needs in abundance." Stop complaining that nothing good ever happens to you and start declaring, "Everything I touch prospers and succeeds." Quit cursing the darkness and instead use your words to bring light into your situation. Your words have that kind of power.

Friend, I trust that this book will help you discover the miracle in your mouth. No matter where you are or what challenges you face, you can start to enjoy a new life filled with abundance as you are transformed and renewed by God's Word.

At the end of every chapter, I have added a short personal reflection. I think you'll see from my commentary that I can't agree more with my father's belief that if we dare to believe God and just act on His Word, the possibilities are endless.

JOEL OSTEEN

The Bible is filled with powerful statements

about who we are in Christ

and what belongs to us as believers.

OVER THE YEARS, I've met countless numbers of people who want to change their lives as well as things in their world. Some of them don't like certain things about themselves or are deeply discouraged about their family life. Others are discontent about their lack of finances and can't seem to ever make ends meet. Many of them can never seem to find relief from chronic illness and pain.

I want you to know that it is possible to change your life as well as things in your world, but it's not by your own efforts. You can change your world by changing your words, and specifically by agreeing with and speaking the Word of God. I have written this book to help you know exactly how to declare the Word of God and experience great changes in your life.

It is my hope that you will not just read this book and then tuck it on a shelf somewhere. Rather, keep it available at all times. Take the scriptural confessions and use them so often that they become your very own. It may seem awkward at first, but if you will faithfully continue to speak God's Word on a daily basis, not only will you be changed, but your circumstances will change.

Life is a battle on many fronts, especially in the spiritual realm. We, as Christians, are constantly engaged in spiritual battles. The Bible teaches us that "we do not wrestle against flesh and blood, but against principalities, against powers, against the rulers of the darkness of this age, against spiritual hosts of wickedness in the heavenly places" (Ephesians 6:12).

God, through Jesus Christ, has totally defeated our enemy, Satan. Second Corinthians 2:14 says, "Now thanks be to God who always leads us in triumph in Christ, and through us diffuses the fragrance of His knowledge in every place." However, a defeated foe does not mean he is not dangerous or any less bent on defeating us.

God has left to us the responsibility of enforcing the victory that Jesus won on the cross and through His resurrection from the dead, and He has armed us with spiritual weapons. "For the weapons of our warfare are not carnal but mighty in God for pulling down strongholds, casting down arguments and every high thing that exalts itself against the knowledge of God, bringing every thought into captivity to the obedience of Christ" (2 Corinthians 10:4–5).

The most powerful weapon God has given us is His Word, and it is my purpose to teach you how to use this weapon. Our lives have many conflicts, but as we learn to use His Word in the same manner that Jesus did when He was tempted by the enemy in the wilderness (Matthew 4:1–11), we will drive the enemy from the field of battle!

Here's the reality: We are this day what we have been continually saying with our mouths in days past. Just think back to what you've been saying about yourself recently, and this will be evident. If you want to change, you must first change your thoughts. Then, in turn, you will change what you speak with your mouth.

In this book I have written some of the most intimate and effective ways I pray and declare God's Word daily. Many times I do not feel or see things as I desire them to be, but I keep on speaking what God has to say about the situation, and these things are brought into reality.

Most of us want to get out of a conflict in the quickest and easiest way possible. None of us enjoy a prolonged battle or struggle. For many, life seems to be a continual struggle. If this is true of your life, this book was written for you especially.

Keep in mind as you read that the changes in our lives may not come instantly. Victory often comes to us gradually. Be patient. The key, as you will learn, is to keep declaring God's Word until the visual image you have of yourself has changed to match the truth of God's Word. This has nothing to do with mind over matter or positive thinking as such. We are dealing with the great eternal promises and the laws of the Word of God.

WHEN YOU BELIEVE GOD'S WORD

in your heart and speak it with your mouth,

God stands behind you

to make it real in your life!

FIND WHAT THE WORD OF GOD SAYS ABOUT YOU

Jesus, the Head of the church, said, *"For assuredly, I say to you, whoever says to this mountain, 'Be removed and be cast into the sea,' and does not doubt in his heart, but believes that those things he says will be done, he will have whatever he says"* (Mark 11:23). This is the heart of the message of this book: Jesus said there is a place you can come to in your relationship with God, if you know the Word of God and don't doubt, where you can have whatever you say! Jesus said you're going to get what you say, so you should be careful about what you say. It is by your words. They have power. Your words are carriers.

Notice that all the way through Jesus' ministry, He found the scriptures that belonged to Him and He spoke those scriptures, knowing the spiritual laws that work. "And as His custom was, He went into the synagogue on the Sabbath day, and stood up to read. And He was handed the book of the prophet Isaiah. And when He had opened the book, *He found the place where it was written:* 'The Spirit of the LORD is upon Me, because He has anointed Me to preach the gospel to the poor; He has sent Me to heal the brokenhearted, to proclaim liberty to the captives and recovery of sight to the blind, to set at liberty those who are oppressed; to proclaim the acceptable year of the LORD.' Then He closed the book, and gave it back to the attendant and sat down. And the eyes of all who were in the synagogue were fixed on Him. And He began to say to them, 'Today this Scripture is fulfilled in your hearing'" (Luke 4:16–21).

The book of Isaiah was handed to Jesus, and He purposefully began to unroll that scroll until He got to Isaiah 61, where Luke says, "He found the place where it was written." Jesus searched the book of Isaiah until He came to the place that specifically spelled out who He was and what He would do. Then He closed the scroll and said with certainty, "I am the One this scripture is written about. This is My scripture, and this is written about Me."

That is precisely what God wants us to do. We must find the places in the Bible that are written about us. Where are those? Simple. The Bible has a wealth of information about believers. God wants us to find scriptures about believers and to boldly declare, "These truths belong to me, and I will have them!"

This is exactly what John the Baptist did. "Now this is the testimony of John, when the Jews sent priests and Levites from Jerusalem to ask him, 'Who are you?' He confessed, and did not deny, but said, 'I am not the Christ.' And they asked him, 'What then? Are you Elijah?' He said, 'I am not.' 'Are you the Prophet?' And he answered, 'No.' Then they said to him, 'Who are you, that we may give an answer to those who sent us? What do you say about yourself?' He said: 'I am

Confessing the Word means to say the same thing as God. It means you take God's powerful Word and make it personal to your life.

"The voice of one crying in the wilderness: Make straight the way of the Lord," as the prophet Isaiah said'" (John 1:19–23). *John gave an answer straight out of the Bible.* He found the place where it was written about him, and he boldly declared, "This is who I am." He didn't say how he felt or how anything else looked. He simply stated, "I am what the Bible says. I am the voice of one crying in the wilderness as the prophet Isaiah said. I'm the voice."

In my own life, after I put my faith in Jesus, for nineteen years I lived and preached to the best of my Christian knowledge. But while I knew my salvation was secure, I didn't really know who I was. Then one day I received the baptism in the Holy Spirit (Acts 2:1–4), and I began to read the New Testament with eyes that were opened. I took off my religious glasses, unplugged my denominational ears, and read the Bible as though I was reading it for the first time. What I saw emerging out of the New Testament was the clear image of a glorious person who shined with a supernatural authority and power that caused the enemy to tremble. And I said, "Oh, God, who is this person that I see coming out of the pages of Scripture?" And the Lord Jesus said, "This is the New Testament believer!"

We need to see ourselves as God sees us! And then we need to begin to speak in the manner God teaches us to speak. We need to dare to find the places in Scripture where it's written about us and declare it as so. And you not only must think it about yourself, you've got to actually say, "It is mine!" You must verbalize it. Your words carry power.

We create our own world around us by the words that we speak. But we just can't choose our own words. We must speak the words out of our mouth that God has spoken in His Word.

Let me make this point crystal clear: *Confessing the Word means to say the same thing as God. It means you take God's powerful Word and make it personal to your life. In faith you agree with God and declare His truths over your life and family. When you agree with God, it shall be done!*

Reflections from
JOEL

In 1981, my mother was diagnosed with cancer and given a few weeks to live. But my mother refused to complain about how sick or weak she felt or how hopeless her situation looked. No, she wrote down ninety-three scriptures she found concerning healing, and all day she would read over them and boldly make declarations such as "With long life, He satisfies me and shows me His salvation" (based on Psalm 91:16). Slowly, week after week, she began to feel better. She kept on confessing God's Word, and more than thirty years later, she remains cancer-free, healed by the power of God and His Word!

My mother used her words to change her world, and you can do the same thing. Your words hold a miracle!

CHAPTER ONE

The Story
of a
Certain
Christian

There was a certain Christian who said he could not, and doubt rose like a giant and conquered him. He talked of failure, and failure became his lot. He spoke continually of sickness, and sickness plagued him. He declared weakness, and he became weaker.

He told all of his friends and family that his debts could never be paid and that he would never have enough money to make it, and poverty moved in to live with him.

He constantly expressed his fear of the past, present, and future, and that fear gripped him. He stated that his marriage was bad and that his children couldn't be controlled, and things just got worse and worse in his household.

He scattered his words everywhere and, like seeds of poison, they grew around him. To hear him talk, he had it very bad. He thought God had treated him unfairly, and that God had left him on his own. *He did not realize he was to blame.*

He did not realize that he, like God, created things with words. It never occurred to him that mankind is the only creation of God that can speak God's powerful thoughts, and thus be a creator *like* his Maker.

THE DISCOVERY OF THE POWER OF GOD'S WORD

One day this Christian found the truth about the power of words in God's Word:

- "Death and life are in the power of the tongue, and those who love it will eat its fruit" (Proverbs 18:21).
- "You are snared by the words of your mouth; you are taken by the words of your mouth" (Proverbs 6:2).
- "For assuredly, I say to you, whoever says to this mountain, 'Be removed and be cast into the sea,' and does not doubt in his heart, but believes that those things he says will be done, he will have whatever he says" (Mark 11:23).

This Christian was amazed at the discovery of this spiritual law: A person creates and brings to pass what he continually says. He also discovered that this law works positively and negatively. He became very aware that it had worked negatively—his whole life proved it. He realized that if his life was going to be different, his words had to change.

What did this Christian do? He began to read his Bible in a new light and saw the great redemptive truths therein. For the first time, he began to *understand* the reason for and the benefits of the death, burial, and resurrection of Jesus. Then he began to see himself as God sees him.

God looked at him and said:

- *You are My child.*
- *You are born again of the incorruptible seed of the Word of God.*
- *You are forgiven of all sin and washed in the blood of Jesus.*
- *You are a new creature—delivered from the power of darkness and translated into My kingdom.*
- *You are redeemed from the curse of the law.*
- *You are blessed and healed by Jesus' stripes.*
- *You are strong in the Lord.*

- *You more than a conqueror.*
- *You are the light of the world and the salt of the earth.*
- *You are the righteousness of God in Christ Jesus.*
- *Greater is He that is in you than he that is in the world.*
- *You have received the power of the Holy Spirit.*
- *You have power to lay hands on the sick and see them recover.*
- *You have power to cast out demons in the Name of Jesus.*
- *You have power over all the power of the enemy.*
- *You can do all things. The works that I do shall you do, and greater works.*
- *You are My ambassador on the earth to tell every creature the Good News of salvation.*
- *I am with you and will never leave you or forsake you.*

This Christian Made a Great Change!

He immediately began to say what God said about him. His words changed, and he declared to God and to man what God said about him. He said it in the face of difficult circumstances, trouble, fear, doubt, and oppression.

He continually said:

- *I am God's child, for I am born of the incorruptible seed of the Word of God.*
- *I am a new creature in Christ Jesus—delivered from the power of darkness and translated into the kingdom of God.*
- *I am redeemed from the curse of the law.*
- *I am blessed and healed by the stripes of Jesus.*
- *I am strong in the Lord.*
- *I am more than a conqueror.*
- *I am the salt of the earth and the light of the world.*
- *I am the righteousness of God in Christ Jesus.*
- *I have the Greater One inside me.*
- *I have received the power of the Holy Spirit.*
- *I have power to lay hands on the sick and see them recover.*
- *I have power to cast out demons in the Name of Jesus.*

- *I have power over all the power of the enemy.*
- *I can do all things through Christ who strengthens me.*
- *I am an ambassador of Jesus Christ to tell the Good News to the world.*
- *I know that God will never leave me or forsake me.*

At first, this Christian made these statements of fact somewhat quietly and timidly. Later, he began to believe in his heart what he spoke with his mouth, and his declarations became bolder and filled with authority.

His friends thought he was foolish. They even felt he was not telling the truth because things did not look any different. They could not see any evidence of change. But this Christian *knew* that he had God's eternal, miracle-working power in his mouth. He *knew* that God's Word is quick and powerful (Hebrews 4:12)! He *knew* that God's Word, spoken out of his mouth, would create the changes he so desperately needed in his life. So he believed in his heart and continually declared the Word of God with his mouth.

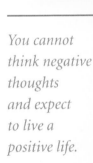

You cannot think negative thoughts and expect to live a positive life.

What God had spoken to Joshua, "This Book of the Law shall not depart from your mouth, but you shall meditate in it day and night, that you may observe to do according to all that is written in it. For then you will make your way prosperous, and then you will have good success" (Joshua 1:8), became a living reality to this Christian!

The apostle Paul explained to us in his letter to the Romans that the Word of God "'is near you, in your mouth and in your heart' (that is, the word of faith which we preach)" (Romans 10:8).

THINGS GREATLY CHANGED!

Change did not happen overnight, but this Christian held fast to his declarations of truth from God's Word. Discouragement and difficulties rose up against him to try to get those words out of his mouth, but the Christian persevered. He knew that God could not lie, and he was determined to partake of all of the blessings of God.

Days and weeks and months went by. Things were the same at first, but they slowly began to change. God's Word began to germinate and to produce fruit.

One day this certain Christian realized that he had:

- *Confidence instead of doubt!*
- *Success instead of failure!*
- *Health instead of sickness!*
- *Strength instead of weakness!*
- *Faith instead of fear!*
- *Courage instead of defeat!*
- *Joy and happiness instead of despair!*

This Christian became a stalwart, courageous soldier of the Lord Jesus Christ. The law of the Spirit of life in Christ Jesus had made him free from the law of sin and death (Romans 8:2).

This Christian had taken the truths of the Word of God, believed them in his heart, spoken them with his mouth, and created his deepest heart's desire.

A PERSON CREATES AND BRINGS TO PASS

what he continually says.

Reflections from
JOEL

A powerful step toward living at your full potential is to discover the power of your thoughts and words. As was true of my father's "certain Christian," many people live far below their full potential because their thinking patterns are defective. You cannot think negative thoughts and expect to live a positive life. You can't think thoughts of failure and expect to succeed.

You've got to quit dwelling on the negative. Don't magnify your problems. Magnify your God. The bigger we make God, the smaller our problems become. Quit dwelling on what's wrong in your life, and start dwelling on what's right in your life. Learn to focus on your possibilities, on what you can do, on your potential. Then go out each day expecting good things.

Friend, if you are going to live your best life now, you must learn how to control your thought life.

CHAPTER TWO

The Power
of the Name
of Jesus

This is a great day to be alive, despite most of the news headlines!

The apostle Paul said that in the closing days before Jesus comes again, "in the last days perilous times will come: For men will be lovers of themselves, lovers of money, boasters, proud, blasphemers, disobedient to parents, unthankful, unholy, unloving, unforgiving, slanderers, without self-control, brutal, despisers of good, traitors, headstrong, haughty, lovers of pleasure rather than lovers of God, having a form of godliness but denying its power" (2 Timothy 3:1–5).

It will be recorded in history that ours has been one of the most turbulent, violent, and shocking generations that has ever lived upon the face of this earth. I believe this is so because the powers of darkness have unleashed its forces upon humanity in an unprecedented manner.

Every level of society feels the power of this evil assault. Alcoholism, drugs, divorces, violence, staggering debt, and overcrowded prisons demonstrate the hopelessness of mankind. Pornography, profanity, and the bold defiance of every good and noble thing we hold dear have arisen like giants to challenge us. Across our land there are men and women who are determined to use every means possible to destroy our heritage—our trust in God—through which our nation was founded.

There has been a monumental loss of faith in government, the monetary system, educational institutions, and the basic social structures that have bound us together. We see our young people driven to every form of excess, with no moral code to hold their lives together. Not finding help in traditional religion and being unable to cope with the sense of hopelessness in the world around them, many have given up and are willing to experiment with anything that comes along!

Where is our God? Where is the God of America? Where is the God of the nations of the world? Where is the mighty Savior of our grandparents? Where is Jesus?

When I went to seminary, I was educated in a church tradition that taught me "The days of miracles are past" and "Divine healing is not for today." Comfortably settled behind stained-glass windows, my Christianity assured us that the powers of darkness were not real, but only a figment of our imagination. In truth, these were lies that held us back from experiencing all that God has provided for us in Christ Jesus!

Today, we who believe on the Lord Jesus Christ boldly declare that the day of miracles is not past! Divine healing for the spirit, mind, and body is available to all! We discern the times in which we live, and we know that the powers of darkness are very real. We are not ignorant.

Has God forgotten to be gracious? Has Jesus forsaken us? No, a thousand times NO! The mighty Miracle Worker, the compassionate Jesus, the Redeemer of all mankind, has manifested Himself with a mighty outpouring of His Holy Spirit even in our days.

While the turbulence of the world roars around us, Jesus walks in our midst. His great power and His great love cannot be hidden. Out of the midst of that murky, profane river of lost humanity, there began to be heard a Name; first on the lips of one, then two, then two hundred, and then thousands upon thousands . . . *the Name of Jesus.* They beheld Him and experienced His love and transforming power, and they were changed forever!

This is why I say this is a great day to be alive! There is mighty power in the Name of Jesus!

IN THE MIGHTY NAME OF JESUS,

God has given us power

to defeat the enemy and stand tall.

JESUS, JESUS, JESUS!

What a sound! Through the blood of Jesus shed on Calvary, the power of darkness, sin, and oppression is broken. Captives are set free by the Name of Jesus.

Today, many of those same young people who were without hope are taking their stand with Jesus. Many people who were broken by divorce, addictions, and abuse in the past have been healed in spirit, mind, and body. They are at the forefront with the message of hope and freedom. Churches of every denomination and all of society have acknowledged Jesus' reality and presence. Jesus is baptizing people in His Holy Spirit and awakening them to the spiritual power He has made available to us.

But God will not do the work for us. He has given us great provisions and weapons: the Holy Spirit, the Name of Jesus, the blood of Jesus, and the Word of God. God intends for us to take our places as His sons and daughters. He wants us to develop ourselves

This Book of the Law shall not depart from your mouth, but you shall meditate in it day and night, that you may observe to do according to all that is written in it.

spiritually. In the mighty Name of Jesus, God has given us power to defeat the enemy and stand tall.

The outpouring of the Holy Spirit has produced spiritual warriors on the earth. Jesus said, "And these signs will follow those who believe: In My name they will cast out demons; they will speak with new tongues; they will take up serpents; and if they drink anything deadly, it will by no means hurt them; they will lay hands on the sick, and they will recover" (Mark 16:17–18).

These believers have taken off their religious masks. They choose to be real! They worship God with their hands lifted high in surrender to Him. They have experienced the grace and ecstasy of the supernatural, based upon the Bible and its redemptive truths. They care about humanity and want to make a difference in people's lives!

And they are coming together, flowing as a mighty river, just as Jesus said they would, and through them God is bringing healing to the nations. Thank God, He has placed within us a river of living water. "On the last day, that great day of the feast, Jesus stood and cried out, saying, 'If anyone thirsts, let him come to Me and drink. He who believes in Me, as the Scripture has said, out of his heart will flow rivers of living water'" (John 7:37–38).

We, as individuals, are not perfect. We make mistakes, but we are being changed. Christ is being formed in us. (See Galatians 4:19.) We are moving swiftly toward the end of time. Soon we will step out of time into eternity.

God has set in the church apostles, prophets, evangelists, pastors, and teachers to bring His people into their rightful place of authority (see Ephesians 4:11–16). He is teaching us how to defeat the enemy. God's servants have been faithfully teaching and training believers throughout the last several years. Because of their faithfulness to the task and the eagerness to learn on the part of God's people, there is being heard the sound of the Name of Jesus!

The sounds of discord, anguish, heartache, confusion, evil, and all sorts of violence, which have dominated the scene and come continually into our ears, are giving way to a new sound, the sound of the Name of Jesus!

We know that we will rise no higher

nor sink lower

THAN OUR CONFESSION OF JESUS.

We Are Not Without Faith

Regarding faith, from the Word of God we know that:

- *"Without faith it is impossible to please Him, for he who comes to God must believe that He is, and that He is a rewarder of those who diligently seek Him"* (Hebrews 11:6).
- *"God has dealt to each one a measure of faith"* (Romans 12:3).
- Jesus is *"the author and finisher of our faith"* (Hebrews 12:2).
- *"Faith comes by hearing, and hearing by the word of God"* (Romans 10:17).
- *"His name, through faith in His name, has made this man strong, whom you see and know. Yes, the faith which comes through Him has given him this perfect soundness in the presence of you all"* (Acts 3:16).

When we take the time to hear the Word of God, that Word will produce in us a steady growth of faith. We will have faith in that Name, and soon we will begin to see as the believers in the New Testament saw. We will see perfect soundness in our bodies.

We always speak out of the abundance of our hearts. Jesus said that a man will bring forth good things out of the good treasure in his heart (see Matthew 12:34–35). We are learning to hear God's Word and to hide it in our hearts. We speak God's Word out of our hearts instead of speaking what we see and feel. This Word of God that is hidden in our hearts and spoken out of our mouths will move mountains in our lives!

We no longer are struggling, but we are taking our place in the Body of Christ as mature men and women of God. We stand confidently, boldly, and unflinchingly in the face of the powers of darkness. We not only refuse to give in to the attacks of Satan on our spirits, minds, and bodies, but we take the offensive and reach out and rescue those around us who have been overcome by the enemy. We do this in the Name of Jesus!

We can be heard everywhere speaking and declaring the promises of God. This is the sound of His Name.

The Sound of the Name of Jesus!

What a refreshing sound it is. We know that we will rise no higher nor sink lower than our confession of Jesus.

The Bible says that the Name of Jesus is above every name! "Therefore God also has highly exalted Him and given Him the name which is above every name, that at the name of Jesus every knee should bow, of those in heaven, and of those on earth, and of those under the earth, and that every tongue should confess that Jesus Christ is Lord, to the glory of God the Father" (Philippians 2:9–11).

When our words have become His Words, every evil force around us must bow to that Name. Jesus has given us the authority to use His Name.

Stop speaking the sound of fear. Stop speaking the sound of depression. Stop speaking the sound of sickness and defeat. Stop speaking of lack and uncertainty.

Make the decision to live your life full of the blessings of God, full of His joy, and full of His peace.

Put on your lips the sound of the Name of Jesus!

Reflections from
JOEL

I met a young woman who described how she lost about two hundred pounds after failing on one diet after another. She said, "One day, I decided to start seeing myself the way I wanted to be—losing the weight and running and playing with my children. I spoke words of victory into my life and said, 'I am well able to lose this weight. I have discipline and self-control. I am more than a conqueror.'" Once that new image of herself showed up on the inside, God could easily develop it on the outside. Today she's living out her dream and enjoying a happier, healthier lifestyle.

You must get an image of what you want to be on the inside first, if you want to see it come to pass in your life on the outside.

CHAPTER THREE

The Power

of Words

Words! Words! Words! There are millions of words in the world. They are written in books, newspapers, on the Internet, and thousands of other places. They are just words.

Then there are words written in the Bible. Thousands of them are there in this "miracle" book. They look just like all the other words in the world. They are spelled the same and sound the same, *but they are different.*

Jesus said, "The words that I speak to you are *spirit,* and they are *life*" (John 6:63). God says His Words "are *life* to those that find them, and *health* to all their flesh" (Proverbs 4:22). He says, "For the word of God is *living* and *powerful,* and *sharper* than any two-edged sword, piercing even to the division of soul and spirit, and of joints and marrow, and is a *discerner* of the thoughts and intents of the heart" (Hebrews 4:12).

The Bible states that "*all scripture is given by inspiration of God,*" or "*God breathed*" (2 Timothy 3:16).

Though the words in the Bible may look the same as those in all the other sources, there is an incredible difference. *They are God's words. God has breathed life into them. When we take these "God-breathed" words and declare them, miracles come to pass!*

Take God's Word and Declare Them

God used words to create this world. He created everything by the word of His power. He created by using words. In Genesis 1, He repeatedly said, "Let there be," and it came into existence.

The words in God's mouth were powerful! Correspondingly, His words spoken by our mouths are also powerful!

What shall you take with you when you turn to the Lord for a miracle? What is it He wants to see you bringing to Him?

- *Hosea 14:2 says,* "Take words with you, and return to the LORD." *Take words! Take God's words! Take God's promises and declare them before Him!*
- *God says,* "Put Me in remembrance" *(Isaiah 43:26). God wants you to remind Him of His promises.*
- *Proverbs 6:2 says,* "You are snared by the words of your mouth; you are taken by the words of your mouth."
- *Jesus says,* "For by your words you will be justified, and by your words you will be condemned" *(Matthew 12:37).*
- *Proverbs 18:21 says,* "Death and life are in the power of the tongue." *I used to say the power of life and death is in the tongue, but I was missing the whole point. That's not what God said. He said,* "Death and life are in the* power *of the tongue." The emphasis is on the power of your tongue.*

Your words are important. You can create hell on earth or heaven on earth with your mouth. You must change your world by changing your words! Put God's words in your mouth and speak them out.

SAY, NOT PRAY

It is important that we pray about our situation, but Joel 3:10 says, "Let the weak say, 'I *am* strong.'" Let the weak *say*—not pray, but *say*.

If the weak are ever to get help, they must change what they are *saying*.

If the troubled are to get help, they must change what they are *saying*.

Let the weak *say* day and night, "The LORD *is* the strength of my life; of whom shall I be afraid?" (Psalm 27:1).

Let the sick *say*, "By His stripes we *are* healed" (Isaiah 53:5). "They will lay hands on the sick, and they *will* recover" (Mark 16:18). Declare, "Hands have been laid on me, and I am recovering. The Lord is my Healer—He has taken sickness from the midst of me." "Bless the LORD, O my soul; and all that is within me, bless His holy name! Bless the LORD, O my soul, and forget not all His benefits: Who *forgives* all [my] iniquities, Who *heals* all [my] diseases" (Psalm 103:1–3). Praise God, He said *all* iniquities and *all* diseases. Faith is agreeing with God and saying what He says about you.

Let the troubled *say* boldly, "God *is* our refuge and strength, a very present help in trouble" (Psalm 46:1). Declare, "God is with me! He is my helper! If God is for me, who can be against me?" "Many are the afflictions of the righteous, but the Lord *delivers* him out of them all" (Psalm 34:19).

Let those who are tormented by fear also change what you are *saying* if you want victory. Let the fearful *say* boldly, day and night, "The Lord *is* my shepherd; I shall not want. Yea, though I walk through the valley of the shadow of death, I will fear no evil; for You *are* with me; Your rod and Your staff, they comfort me" (Psalm 23:1, 4). Speak out the word, "I fear not for You are with me. I am not dismayed for You are my God. You are *helping me!* You are *strengthening me!* You are upholding me with the right hand of Your righteousness" (see Isaiah 41:10)!

Let the fearful *say* over and over again, "The Lord *is* my light and my salvation; whom shall I fear? The Lord *is* the strength of my life; of whom shall I be afraid? When the wicked came against me to eat up my flesh, my enemies and foes, they stumbled and fell" (Psalm 27:1–2).

Let those who are haunted by fear *say*, "For God has not given us a spirit of fear, but of power and of love and of a sound mind" (2 Timothy 1:7). Declare it so! "I have no spirit of fear. I have the Holy Spirit of power! I have the spirit of love! I have the spirit of a sound mind!" Declare this to everyone. Don't talk about your fears; talk about what God says about you. Act the part as you speak the truth of God's Word, and fear will melt away like the mist before the rising sun.

Let the weak *say*!

Let the troubled *say*!

Let the sick *say*!

Let the fearful *say*!

Let those in need of victory *say*!

YOU MUST CHANGE YOUR WORLD
BY CHANGING YOUR WORDS!
*Put God's words in your mouth
and speak them out.*

What Shall You *Say*?

What shall we say? *Say what God says!* It's as simple as that! Take His promises and climb up to His throne, through the Lord Jesus, and "put Him in remembrance." Declare that the promises of God are coming to pass right now.

Hebrews 13:5–6 says, "For He Himself has said, 'I will never leave you nor forsake you.' So we may boldly say: 'The Lord is my helper; I will not fear. What can man do to me?'" This is a most remarkable scripture!

Notice that it says, *"He Himself has said, . . . So we may boldly say."*

God has given us hundreds of promises in His Word to *believe*, then to *boldly speak them in our declaration for deliverance.*

Search the Scriptures for one of His promises that fits your situation. Believe it in your heart. Now start to *boldly speak this promise* to yourself, your friends, your family, and to the enemy! *Boldly* declare to all, "This is what God, my Father, has said, and I believe it! It is mine now!" Hold on to it and declare it in pain, trouble, fear, sickness, and need. Jesus is the "High Priest of our confession," and He will surely see that it becomes a reality in your life.

If you don't think this spiritual law of speaking God's Word works, try it in reverse. That's what most people do anyway. First, they believe they are sick and are certain they are going to get worse. They tell everyone about it. Ask them, and they will say clearly and convincingly, "I am sick. I hurt. I probably will have to go to the hospital. This thing is getting worse." On and on they go. They believe it and speak it, *and they get what they speak!*

If it works in reverse, surely it works in forward motion. *It works when we exercise faith to declare God's promises and truths about our lives.*

So begin today. Do not doubt. Believe in your heart what God has said about you in His Word and speak it out constantly, and *you shall have whatever you say* (see Mark 11:23).

You see, *God watches over His Word to perform it* (see Jeremiah 1:12). This is a spiritual law grounded in His Word.

What shall we say?
Say what God says!
It's as simple as that!

WHAT VOICE ARE YOU LISTENING TO?

There are three voices that talk to you:

- *First,* the voice from this present world, which is controlled by "the rulers of the darkness of this age" (Ephesians 6:12), cries out when disease, financial instability, relationship problems, addictions, and general woes come into your life. It cries out in powerful and thundering tones: "You're sick! You're in trouble! You won't make it! You can't change!" That's one voice.

- *Second,* the voice from God in His Word tells us, "By His stripes we are healed. He bore our sicknesses. He took our curse, being made a curse for us. He bore our sins" (see Isaiah 53:4–5). "My God shall supply your every need" (see Philippians 4:19). Symptoms and circumstances say one thing, but God says another thing. The whole crux of the matter is . . .

- *Third,* what are you going to say about it? Whose side are you going to take? Are you going to throw in the towel and agree with what people are saying about your life or what you have been saying about your life? Or will you take your stand on the Word of God and declare what God has said?

Let me remind you, the Bible says, "Let the weak *say*," not *pray*. "Let the weak say, 'I am strong'" (Joel 3:10). That's what God says. The weak must say something. Let the sick say, "I am healed." Let the troubled say, "I am delivered." Let the oppressed and bound say, "I am free." Let the discouraged say, "I am filled with hope." *Say it on the basis of the truths of the Word of God.*

One of the most astonishing discoveries I have found in the Bible is about words! Consider the woman who secretly came to Jesus with the issue of blood. She said something! In Matthew 9:21, she *said* to herself, "If only I may touch His garment, I shall be made well."

Look at David as he faced Goliath. He said something! David *said*, "This day the Lord will deliver you into my hand, and I will strike you and take your head from you" (1 Samuel 17:46).

The woman of Canaan (a Gentile) came in desperation to Jesus for her demon-possessed daughter, and Jesus wouldn't listen to her there (see Matthew 15:22–27). He wasn't being rude; His purpose was to increase her faith. As she followed after Him, He wouldn't answer her pleas. The disciples said, "Send her away, for she cries out after us." She *said*, "O Lord, Son of David! My daughter is severely demon-possessed." The mother of this daughter was coming after Jesus, crying out for help, wanting a miracle for the little daughter who was at home in need. Finally, Jesus turned and said, "It is not good to take the children's bread and throw it to the little dogs." And she *said*, "Yes, Lord, yet even the little dogs eat the crumbs which fall from their masters' table."

Now listen to this! Jesus said, *"O woman, great is your faith! Let it be to you as you desire"* (Matthew 15:28). Think about it! This Gentile woman could speak words of faith and bring deliverance and wholeness to her daughter. Because of what she had said in faith, Jesus told her that her daughter was free!

In contrast, how many of us get ourselves into trouble because of things we *say*. When we say that we just can't believe, when we say we don't receive, when we say we do not yield, and when we say we're going to do this, that, and the other thing that is contrary to God, we are agreeing with the powers of darkness.

This lone woman of Canaan came to Jesus, worshiping Him and *saying*. Her daughter was many miles away from her. Jesus said that the declaration of her words was so powerful that she possessed healing for her daughter.

It really is that important what you say!

THE MIRACLE IS IN YOUR MOUTH

Did you know that you are now a composite of what you've been saying? You possess in your body, in your mind, in your physical being, and in your spiritual being what you've been saying. If you're weak and defeated, check yourself. You are the product of what you have been saying, because you receive what you say. If you want to become different, you must change what you are saying. If you want to change your life, you have to change your words to align with God's Word.

The miracle is in *your* mouth. No minister can help you if you persist in agreeing with the messages of this world. No one can help you if you will not speak what God has said in His Word.

IF YOU WANT TO BECOME DIFFERENT,

you must change what you are saying.

Reflections from
JOEL

Our words have tremendous power and are similar to seeds. By speaking them aloud, they are planted in our subconscious minds, take root, grow, and produce fruit of the same kind. Whether we speak positive or negative words, we will reap exactly what we sow. That's why we need to be extremely careful what we think and say.

The Bible compares the tongue to the small rudder of a huge ship, which controls the ship's direction (see James 3:4). Similarly, your tongue will control the direction of your life. You create an environment for either good or evil with your words, and if you're always murmuring, complaining, and talking about how bad life is treating you, you're going to live in a pretty miserable world.

Use your words to change your negative situations and fill them with life.

CHAPTER FOUR

The ABCs

of

Faith

There is no limit to what a Christian can do for God no matter where he or she is, if he or she will learn the ABCs of faith, dare to believe God, and just act on His Word.

However, our problem often starts when we think we can understand God's principles with our intellect. While the intellect is certainly important, know this: You understand spiritual principles *by faith*.

Hebrews 11:3 tells us, "*By faith we understand* that the worlds were framed by the word of God, so that the things which are seen were not made of things which are visible." What is seen? The stars, the moon, the sun, the earth, the trees, the flowers, the clouds, etc. And what we see was made out of invisible things. We believe in an invisible, unseen God who made all that we see, and we believe by faith. Our minds can never comprehend God or His creation of all things.

One day my daughter Tamara asked me, "Daddy, where did God come from?" I answered, "Darling, don't trouble your mind about that. You may learn that in eternity."

There are a lot of things you are not going to understand with your mind. It is through faith that you understand.

You may say, "I just don't know how I will ever be successful or obtain financial blessing. I don't see how it can happen." It is through faith you can understand.

A lot of people want to *try* faith. But faith is not a formula to try in emergencies. Faith is a way of life. And as we read in Hebrews 11:7, "But without faith it is impossible to please Him, for he who comes to God must believe that He is, and that He is a rewarder of those who diligently seek Him," this is not a chance statement. It is a fact of God's Word that it is not possible to please God without faith. It makes no difference what you do, what you say, or how good you live, you cannot please God unless you are functioning in faith.

If we have just a grain of the God-kind of faith, Jesus said nothing shall be impossible to us (Matthew 17:20)!

Do you dare to believe that? Jesus sees the possibilities of our lives. You do not have to be a spiritual giant and have a lot of faith. But you must learn to exercise your faith.

"A"—Agree With the Word of God

After what I have just said about faith, this statement may confound you: *Do not worry about having faith.* Don't look all around trying to find faith as so many Christians do. They make faith so mechanical and complicated that they miss it.

Just as you cannot analyze love, you cannot analyze faith. I love my wife, Dodie. I remember when I first fell in love with her. I saw her standing out by the church where I was pastoring. I had known her for a long time, but at that time I said to myself, "That little thing doesn't know it yet, but I am going to marry her." There were choices involved, of course, but I could never dissect or analyze why I felt so wonderful when I saw her. Why did my heart turn over three times and pat, pat, pat, real fast? Where did the emotions come from? Why did I want to be with her all the time? Why?

I found that I could not analyze love. Love was just there. I merely had to enjoy it!

It is the same with faith. *Don't worry about having faith.* Just start with the basic element of faith . . . *agree with the Word of God.*

Get rid of the notion that faith is a strange or mystical thing. Agree with what the Bible says: God has given you the measure of faith (Romans 12:3). Accept it as fact, and go on to grow in the principles of God.

This is just as true for me as it is for you. Over and over again, I have to be reminded of how faith works. In my life, often when I have been "down in the valley" of discouragement, Dodie has looked me right in the face and said, "John, declare the Word of God! Open your mouth and say . . ."

If you do it, it will work for you! You must agree with what the Word says about you.

What do I mean by that? Here are some familiar scriptural examples for how you can agree with the Word of God.

- *"I believe and agree with Romans 10:9–10, which states, 'If you confess with your mouth the Lord Jesus and believe in your heart that God has raised Him from the dead, you will be saved. For with the heart one believes unto righteousness, and with the mouth confession is made unto salvation.' Whether I feel saved or not, I agree with the Word of God. I confess Jesus as my Lord, and God says that I am saved. Therefore, I agree with His Word: I am saved. I have peace with God."* The greatest miracle in the world is wrought by believing in your heart and saying with your mouth that Jesus is your Lord and that God raised Him from the dead!

- *Agree with God that you are a new creature in Christ Jesus. "I agree with 2 Corinthians 5:17: 'Therefore, if anyone is in Christ, he is a new creation; old things have passed away; behold, all things have become new.' I am a new creature in Christ. My past is forgiven, and I am a child of God. I agree with the Bible. I thank God I am a new creature."*

- *Agree with God that you are delivered from the power of darkness. "I agree with Colossians 1:13: 'He has delivered us from the power of darkness and conveyed us into the kingdom of the Son of His love.' No matter how it looks, or how I feel, or what the enemy accuses me of, I declare that I have been delivered from the power and the authority of the kingdom of darkness. I agree with God. He says that I am delivered from Satan's power, and I agree."* That will put the enemy on tranquilizers!

- *There was a time in my life when if I did something wrong, I felt so badly that I would go for days under a cloud of condemnation. I didn't feel worthy to preach or pray. Finally, after days of feeling condemned, I would accept my forgiveness. But I didn't have to wait, and neither do you.*

   When you make a mistake and you sin, just say, "Father, I am guilty. Your Word says, 'If I confess my sins, You are faithful and just to forgive my sins, and to cleanse me from all unrighteousness' (see 1 John 1:8–9). I agree with that scripture. I have confessed my sins, and You have kept Your end of the bargain. Therefore, no matter what I have done, I am cleansed by the blood of Jesus from all unrighteousness. I will not be under a cloud of condemnation about it. I agree with what Your Word says, and I am cleansed!"

Faith is not a formula to try in emergencies.

FAITH IS A WAY OF LIFE.

- *In regards to physical, emotional, or mental healing, you can agree with 1 Peter 2:24 that "by [Jesus'] stripes you are healed." No matter what your body says, you can say, "I agree with God. By Jesus' stripes I am healed."* When you are sick and hurting, it is hard to try to feel healed. Do not worry about having faith. *Look at the scriptures and say, "I agree." When you hear a voice saying, "You will never be well," point to the Bible and say, "No, I agree with God. He cannot lie. His Word says, 'By His stripes I am healed.' And I simply agree with God."*

The "A" of Faith Is Agree With the Word of God.

"B"—BELIEVE THE WORD OF GOD

When you believe the Word of God, you must act like it is so. This does not mean I do some foolish thing to prove that God will take care of me. For instance, just because God says He has given His angels charge over me, doesn't mean I must jump off of a building as the devil tried to get Jesus to do in the temptation in the wilderness (Matthew 4:1–11). Don't let the enemy push you into some foolish area.

When you act on the Word, you act like it is so. James 1:22 says, "But be doers of the word, and not hearers only, deceiving yourselves." The only Word that will do you any good is that Word you act upon. It is better to take only one scripture and act like it is true than to do nothing. If you diligently read and study the Word of God, get it into your spirit and put it into practice, *it will work.*

This truth has brought health to both Dodie and me. Dodie was diagnosed with metastatic cancer of the liver in 1981 and was given only a few weeks to live. She did not get well by agreeing with the medical verdict that she would not recover. She got well when she took the Word of God and declared that what it said about healing was true.

In my life, at one time it seemed as though I had lost my ministry. I was so sick and discouraged that it looked as though I was not going to make it. I am telling you that *doing the Word*—acting like it is so—brought me out and set my feet on solid ground.

I am not talking about this in theory. I am talking about something that I know works.

You may say, "Well, how can I act like the Word is so?"

Consider what Noah did when he heard God say, "There is going to be a flood." He didn't say, "I've got faith. I am the greatest man in the world, and I have faith." No! Noah did not worry about having faith. He just agreed with God that there was a flood coming, and then he acted like it was so and started building the ark. Noah did not have to say, "I have faith that a flood is coming." The very fact that he was sawing timbers and hammering on the boat told his story. Noah demonstrated his faith by his works.

Read through Hebrews 11. We're told there that Abraham heard from God, and by faith he acted like God told him the truth. Moses acted like God told him the truth. Abel, Enoch, Noah, Sarah, Isaac, Joseph, and Jacob heard God's Word, and they acted like it was so *through faith*.

There are practical ways that you can act like the Word of God is true. I have three sweet "P"s to help you act like the Word is so.

"P" Number One: PRAISE

By praise, you can act like God's Word is true. You act by praising.

If God said, "You shall live and not die," and you walk around like a "corpse" twenty-four hours a day for six months, you are showing by your actions that you do not believe God.

Let's suppose that Jesus literally appeared to you in person, looked you right in the eyes, and said, "I want you to see Me with your eyes. Now listen to these words: By My stripes you are healed." You would run up and down wherever you were and tell everybody what you saw and heard. "I am healed! Thank God, I am healed. The Word of God says that I am healed."

Let me tell you something: The Word of God that is written in the Bible is just as powerful and true as if Jesus stood before you and spoke you the Word. When you read the Bible, find the scripture that relates to the area of your need—whether it is financial, emotional, mental, physical, or a marital problem—and agree with what the Word says about it. Then begin to praise God and act like it is so. Say, "Oh, thank You, Father. I agree with that scripture."

It may seem as though every power of darkness is assailing your mind, telling you that it is not so. "Your husband is never going to come into the family of God. Your son and daughter are never going to believe in Jesus. Your family problem is never going to work out."

Those are the enemy's lies. Just stand there in the midst of it and say, "I praise You, Father, and I agree with Your Word. I praise You that Your Word is true." When you do this, you are showing that you are acting on the Word and believing it . . . *by your praise!*

The Lord desires that we praise Him.

Second Chronicles 20 records the account of an overwhelmingly large army of Moabites, Ammonites, and others coming against Jehoshaphat, the king of Judah. It looked as though Judah was doomed. All of Judah cried out to God. We read in verses 13–15: "Now all Judah, with their little ones, their wives, and their children, stood before the LORD. Then the Spirit of the LORD came upon Jahaziel the son of Zechariah, the son of Benaiah, the son of Jeiel, the son of Mattaniah, a Levite of the sons of Asaph, in the midst of the assembly. And he said, 'Listen, all you of Judah and you inhabitants of Jerusalem, and you, King Jehoshaphat! Thus says the LORD to you: "Do not be afraid nor dismayed because of this great multitude, for the battle is not yours, but God's."'"

We don't have to fight the enemy; he is already defeated. *The greatest and only battle that we must fight is the fight of faith.* God adds in verse 17: "'You will not need to fight in this battle. Position yourselves, stand still and see the salvation of the LORD, who is with you, O Judah and Jerusalem!' Do not fear or be dismayed; tomorrow go out against them, for the LORD is with you."

We read in verse 18 that all the inhabitants fell before the Lord and worshiped Him. *The first thing we are going to have to do is praise God.* Verse 22 tells us what God did when they were willing to sing and praise Him. "Now when they began to sing and to praise, the LORD set ambushes against the people of Ammon, Moab, and Mount Seir, who had come against Judah; and they were defeated."

When we begin to praise God because He said that the battle is His and His promises are ours, God begins to work. There in the spiritual world, God smites the enemy and brings victory.

If you diligently read and study the Word of God,

GET IT INTO YOUR SPIRIT

AND PUT IT INTO PRACTICE, IT WILL WORK.

In the natural, Jehoshaphat had no chance. His army was outnumbered in every way. And yet God said, "It's all right; I am going to bring you through. The battle is Mine." I believe that when their choir came out and they offered God their praise, God said to Gabriel, "Look at that! They know that they don't have a chance, but they actually believe Me. Look at them praising Me. We can't let them down. They are acting like I told them the truth. Gabriel, go and strike their enemies."

God set them free because they had learned how to praise Him.

You may say, "I don't have much to praise God for. My pocketbook and bank account are empty." That is when you should say, "Oh, I praise God. You have promised to supply all of my needs (Philippians 4:19). Everything I put my hand to prospers and succeeds! Thank God!"

Paul and Silas had been beaten with rods and thrown into prison, but they responded in faith (Acts 16:25) and brought salvation to the keeper of the prison and his household.

When we begin to praise God because He said that the battle is His and His promises are ours, God begins to work.

Abraham grew strong in faith as he gave glory to God. He praised the Lord. We can read about it in Romans 4:3: "For what does the Scripture say? 'Abraham believed God, and it was accounted to him for righteousness.'" He had the God-kind of faith: "(as it is written, 'I have made you a father of many nations') in the presence of Him whom he believed—God, who gives life to the dead and calls those things which do not exist as though they did" (vv. 17–20).

You can do that in every situation: Praise God!

"P" Number Two: PLAN

You can show that you believe the Word of God and that you are acting on that Word by the plans you make.

Some people who have diseases in their bodies say they believe that by the stripes of Jesus they are healed, yet they make plans to die. Others make plans as though they will never be able to go anywhere or do anything outside their homes. If you listen to the lies of the enemy, he will have you making plans to fail.

Have you ever said, "There is no use in planning to take a vacation. We are just barely getting along. We never have had much. We can't make plans for a vacation!" Go ahead. Make those plans for a vacation. God is not broke.

Perhaps you're saying, "You must be crazy! I don't even have enough money to pay my utilities, and here you're suggesting I plan a vacation?"

Rather, say this: "Yes, I am acting on my faith." I make my plans to live as though God told me the truth. God cannot lie.

You may say, "Pastor Osteen, how can I make plans? What is it that you suggest that I do?"

First: Decide what it is that you want to do. What are you believing God for? What is it you want to see changed in your life?

Then, act like it is so—by making plans to live a good, healthy, glorious, Spirit-filled, abundant, active life. If you make your plans that way, God will make your plans come true. For instance, if you are having trouble in your business, go ahead and make your plans to increase its size.

I am always making plans for our church. I once looked outside of our little church that seated 234 people, and I said, "Look out there." Everybody turned and looked at the wall. I said, "There is a Chinese store sitting over there, but I see a church seating 1,000 people. I am making plans."

Every service we would turn and look and make our confession for a larger church. Visitors who came in would look at us and say, "You're crazy! You all look at the wall and say, 'We see a church over there!'"

We made our plans as though God meant it when He said, "Enlarge the place of your tent, and let them stretch out the curtains of your dwellings" (Isaiah 54:2). And God helped our plans. At first we did not have enough money to buy a saltshaker. We couldn't even start to take the tin off the side of the building and put brick on it. But we made our plans as though we were one of the wealthiest churches. We acted as though our Father said the truth when He said, "My God shall supply all of your needs." Thank God, when we made our plans, we finally raised $7,000, which seemed like seven million dollars at the time. That was enough to pour the foundation.

One day a friend of mine came by and said, "Why don't you build that building out there?"

I said, "We have only enough money to pour the foundation."

He said, "Why don't you go ahead and pour that foundation? Every journey begins with one step." He was right.

If you are in your car at night and want to go home, you turn on the headlights and are only able to see about fifty yards. If you say, "Well, I'm not going to move until I can see all the way home," you won't get far. No! You have to take each step by faith. You have to drive in the fifty yards of light that you have. When you do that, you will see fifty yards more, and fifty yards more, and fifty yards more.

Thank God, we took our $7,000 and poured the foundation for a larger church. When we spent that, we had more, and more, and more. God helped us, and we have continued to grow and grow. We enlarged our auditorium three times before building a new 8,200-seat auditorium in 1988. Then in 1991, we dedicated a two-story, 37,000-square-foot Children's Center. And we kept building.

In one month in 1980, we gave $103,000 to missions. The following year, we gave nearly two million dollars. In the decade after 1981, we more than doubled our missionary endeavors all over the world.

You may say, "Well, when are you going to stop?"

Never. Because with God there is no limit. So plan accordingly.

"P" Number Three: PARTICIPATE

As you praise God and make your plans, you must also participate. Participation is how you show that you believe the Word of God. You agree with the Word of God. You believe the Word of God. And you act like it is so by praising, by your plans, and by your participation. You must participate in what you ordinarily cannot do.

If it is financial, participate in the giving. If you only have a dime, give something! Give, even if it is a penny.

There was a time when Dodie and I did not have enough money to pay our debts. One time, before we had children, we only had enough money to buy one sandwich. We bought it, divided the sandwich, and ate it. Then we learned to start giving. Thank God, He has prospered us.

Start this way. If it is a physical need, and you cannot do much physically, start doing a little bit. If you say, "I can't run the one-hundred-yard dash," run a "hundred-inch dash." Begin as fast as you can. Start with a foot, two feet, then a yard, two yards, then three. Start doing a little bit of what you cannot do.

"C"—Confess the Word With Your Mouth

Under the ABCs of Faith, you must *Agree* with the Word, then *Believe* the Word and act like it is so through your Praise, Plans, and Participation. We now come to *Confess*.

The power of life and death is in *your* tongue. You must declare the Word of God.

This is the basic principle that we speak out loud: "I confess that I believe what God says."

In the Introduction, I wrote how John the Baptist found and confessed the Old Testament prophecy concerning his life and ministry. He made it absolutely clear that he was "the voice of one crying in the wilderness: Make straight the way of the Lord," as Isaiah had said (John 1:23).

In the previous verses, we read where the priests and Levites asked John the Baptist, "Who are you? Are you Elijah? Are you the Prophet?" He said, "No." And he gave them the entire record of how Jesus was Lord, and how he was unworthy to untie His shoelaces (see John 1:26–27).

But I want to call your attention to a question that they asked him. I believe this is one of the most important questions in the Bible, for John that day and for every believer today. *"What do you say about yourself?"* (v. 22).

If someone asked you, "Who are you? What do you say about yourself?" what would be your answer? Would you say, "Well, thank you for asking, but I'm just another guy who lives down the road. I don't have an education, and I come from a dysfunctional family. No one in my family has been a success, and neither will I. God said He wants to bless me, but I guess I am the exception."

"What do you say about yourself?" "Well, I am just barely making it. They say that God will supply all of my needs in Christ Jesus, but I can't even pay my debts. I don't get how it works, but I can't afford to give when they take up an offering."

Have you ever heard people talk that way? Do you talk that way?

"What do you say about yourself?"

I don't know how John the Baptist felt when he was asked that question. I suspect that he wasn't in the best of moods, because on that same day he called the Pharisees and Sadducees "a brood of vipers" (Matthew 3:7). Let's suppose that he was all out of sorts; that he didn't have much money to buy locusts and wild honey. Then when they came to him and said, "What do you say about yourself?" he could have given them quite an answer!

But John confined what came out of his mouth to what the Bible said about him. He said, "I am the voice that Isaiah the prophet spoke about." He could well have said, "I am not going to tell you anything about myself except what God says about me."

That is precisely what we need to do. We should say about ourselves what God says. "I am successful." "I am strong." "I am blessed."

Thank God, we are what God says we are.

I have a friend by the name of Bob Buess. He used to be so bashful that he wouldn't even get up on the platform with me. Now he is as bold as a lion and has a real unique ministry. He told me about a woman who wrote him page after page of all the bad things about herself. "I am this . . . I am that . . . this is the way I am, and nobody likes me." After she had finished berating herself, she said, "Can you help me?"

Bob wrote back and said, "After reading your letter, I don't like you either! How could anybody like you when you speak these things about yourself?" He talked to her about her negativity and explained that because of it, she had talked him into not liking her. Then he told her how to speak what God says.

Your mouth can get you into trouble or it can get you out of trouble. You should speak what God says about you.

Thank God, we are what God says we are.

I am the sum total of what I have been declaring through the years. My children are the best children that ever lived on the face of the earth. They are blessed of God. They are the sum total of what Dodie and I have declared and loved them into being.

Confess the Word of God instead of negative things. You may ask, "How long do I have to confess it?" All of your life. In every situation, do these things:

A—Agree with the Word of God. Don't worry about having faith.

B—Believe the Word of God. Act like it is so—by your praise, by your plans, and by your participation.

C—Confess the Word of God with your mouth.

As you act on these principles, you may not be without battles, *but you will never lose the war.* These are simple steps in living a victorious Christian life. Begin today to apply these principles in every area of your life, and as you do, you will experience God's power and provision at work for you.

Reflections from
JOEL

*W*hen David faced the giant Goliath, he didn't complain and say, "God, why do I always have huge problems?" He didn't dwell on the fact that Goliath was three times his size or that Goliath was a skilled warrior and he was just a shepherd boy. Rather than focus on the magnitude of the obstacle before him, David chose to focus on the greatness of God.

David looked Goliath right in the eyes and spoke aloud these words of faith: "You come against me with sword and spear and javelin, but I come against you in the name of the LORD Almighty, the God of the armies of Israel, whom you have defied" (1 Samuel 17:45). He didn't merely think them; he didn't simply pray them, but he spoke directly to his mountain (Goliath) and brought him down.

CHAPTER FIVE

Seven Things
We Have
in Christ

nce we have received salvation, we must grow in our knowledge of God and His Word because He has given us numerous promises and blessings that He desires for us to experience. Salvation is the greatest gift to mankind, but it is also just the beginning of a life of victory.

The apostle Peter reminds us that we, as believers, should be like newborn babies who crave spiritual milk so that we will grow up and mature in our salvation (1 Peter 2:2).

The Bible says, "Now we have received, not the spirit of the world, but the Spirit who is from God, that we might know the things that have been freely given to us by God" (1 Corinthians 2:12). Paul states four important truths in this passage of Scripture:

1. *We have not received the spirit of the world.*
2. *We have received the Spirit that is of God.*
3. *We have received the Holy Spirit that we might know the things God has given us.*
4. *God has freely given us blessings.*

Yes, thanks be to God because He has given us His Spirit that we might *know*. His Spirit will take us beyond believing into *knowing*.

Unfortunately, as was true of me for the first nineteen years of my Christian life, many believers deny the fullness of the work of the Holy Spirit today. Generally, this is followed by a lack of faith, a lack of spiritual victory, a lack of using the wonderful Name of Jesus, and a lack of receiving the blessings freely given to us of God. It was only when the Lord Jesus baptized me in the Holy Spirit that I truly began to understand what God had freely given to me. Even so, there is a continual unfolding of the Lord Jesus Christ, and I have not arrived!

Approximately four years before his death, the apostle Paul exhibited in his letter to the Philippians a perfect spirit and example for us to follow: ". . . that I may know Him and the power of His resurrection, and the fellowship of His sufferings, being conformed to His death" (Philippians 3:10).

My prayer is that I might *know* Jesus and the power of His resurrection. I have not yet begun to know Him as I want to know Him. *I want to know Jesus* "in whom are hidden all the treasures of wisdom and knowledge" (Colossians 2:3). These treasures, these blessings, are hidden in Him.

My prayer is for you to know Jesus in a greater capacity. I desire for you to know the many blessings that are available to you because you belong to Christ Jesus.

Partake of the Blessings!

In 2 Kings 7, the Bible tells a remarkable story. While a large Syrian army had camped outside the city gates of Samaria, the people within the city were starving. They were so desperate that they were actually eating their own babies. There was no food, and death was everywhere.

"Now there were four leprous men at the entrance of the gate; and they said to one another, 'Why are we sitting here until we die?' And they rose at twilight to go to the camp of the Syrians; and when they had come to the outskirts of the Syrian camp, to their surprise no one was there. For the LORD had caused the army of the Syrians to hear the noise of chariots and the noise of horses—the noise of a great army; so they said to one another, 'Look, the king of Israel has hired against us the kings of the Hittites and the kings of the Egyptians to attack us!'

"Therefore they arose and fled at twilight, and left the camp intact—their tents, their horses, and their donkeys—and they fled for their lives. And when these lepers came to the outskirts of the camp, they went into one tent and ate and drank, and carried from it silver and gold and clothing, and went and hid them; then they came back and entered another tent, and carried some from there also, and went and hid it. Then they said to one another, 'We are not doing right. This day is a day of good news, and we remain silent. If we wait until morning light, some punishment will come upon us. Now therefore, come, let us go and tell the king's household.' Then the people went out and plundered the tents of the Syrians. So a seah of fine flour was sold for a shekel, and two seahs of barley for a shekel, according to the word of the LORD" (2 Kings 7:3, 5–9, 16).

Notice the *first* thing these lepers did? They *said* to one another, "Why are we sitting here until we die?"

The *second* thing they did was move. They *rose up.* When they acted, God did something for them.

Third, the lepers *moved* toward the enemy. God caused the great host of the Syrian army to hear a noise of chariots, then to flee in terror, leaving all their supplies.

In the city of Samaria, people were starving. They had no hope. Beyond the city walls, food was available, but they did not have *knowledge* of it. The lepers, however, were eating because they said something, rose up, and moved toward the enemy!

Now I want to say what God's Word says. Why are you sitting here until you die? Rise up! Go toward those encamped against you, and the enemy will flee from you in terror! Some of us have left the camp and gone after the enemy. We have been to the household of the King, and we can tell you, *the famine is over!*

Yes, there is a universal call on humanity through Jesus Christ! "Ho! Everyone who thirsts, come to the waters; and you who have no money, come, buy and eat. Yes, come, buy wine and milk without money and without price" (Isaiah 55:1).

Thank God, He is pouring out His Spirit upon all flesh. Living water is available to all without measure. You may be facing a death sentence from some dreadful disease. You may be facing a great disappointment. Rise up in your spirit. Use God's Word as a weapon. God's Spirit will enforce His Word, and it will be *according to the Word of the Lord.*

Do you know what I see? I see God's people remaining behind religious walls, walls of tradition, and walls of ignorance to the Word of God. They do not know what God has already freely given to them.

I come to tell you, "The famine is over. Yes, come, buy wine and milk without money and without price." Jesus paid the price—and it was not cheap. The price He paid includes anything that we will ever need as long as we are on the earth. The price He paid includes eternal life with Him.

Whether you are already a member of the household of the King or have never heard the message of salvation, God wants you to partake of the blessings that He has freely given you. Perhaps you have sat in the city and never enjoyed your blessings. You may be starving to death, but the blessings are yours! If you have received Jesus Christ, you are of the household of the King!

Let's look at seven things that are ours in Christ.

1. WE ARE SAVED IN CHRIST

The first thing we have in Christ is salvation. I want you to boldly say, *"I am saved."*

You may say, "I already know I am saved." Well, it is good to know it again. Many people know they are saved today, but tomorrow when they stumble and sin, they think, *Well, I wouldn't dare say I am saved now.*

There is an assurance and a stability that every child of God can have. You can say without a doubt, "I know I am saved. My sins have been forgiven, and I have peace with God."

Don't doubt God's love and promises to you. Don't insult God by speaking words contrary to the truth. Some believers say, "I am just an old sinner." That's not what God's Word says about you! God has forgiven you, accepted you, and saved you by His great mercy and grace. "But what does it say? 'The word is near you, in your mouth and in your heart' (that is, the word of faith which we preach): that if you confess with your mouth the Lord Jesus and believe in your heart that God has raised Him from the dead, you will be saved. For with the heart one believes unto righteousness, and with the mouth confession is made unto salvation. For the Scripture says, 'Whoever believes on Him will not be put to shame'" (Romans 10:8–11).

Now you say: "I confess with my mouth that Jesus is my Lord. I believe in my heart that God raised Him from the dead. Therefore, *I am saved!*"

Did God promise that? Yes. God *said it!* You are not speaking something that you made up. You are not saying something based on your own feelings. You are declaring what God Himself has said. When you believe in your heart that God raised Jesus from the dead and confess that He is your Lord, you have a Bible right to say, *I am saved!*

Have you received Jesus as your Lord? "But as many as received Him, to them He gave the right to become children of God, to those who believe in His name" (John 1:12). If you confess that you have received Him, this passage of Scripture is speaking about *you*. God gave you the power (the authority and right) to become sons of God. You are a child of God.

If anyone ever questions your right to say that you are a child of God, remember that according to Romans 10:9–10, you can boldly declare: "I confess with my mouth

> *Use God's Word as a weapon. God's Spirit will enforce His Word, and it will be according to the Word of the Lord.*

that Jesus is my Lord. I believe in my heart that God raised Him from the dead. Therefore, I am saved." And according to John 1:12, "Because I have received Jesus, I am a child of God." Therefore, you can boldly say that God has given you the authority and the right to be known as a son or a daughter of God.

God wants us to know that we are saved. "For God so loved the world that He gave His only begotten Son, that whoever believes in Him should not perish but have everlasting life. For God did not send His Son into the world to condemn the world, but that the world through Him might be saved" (John 3:16–17). He wants us to know that we are His children. "Most assuredly, I say to you, he who hears My word and believes in Him who sent Me has everlasting life, and shall not come into judgment, but has passed from death into life" (John 5:24).

Perhaps you are waiting to die to see if you pass the test. I want to tell you, "You have already passed out of death into life! You have confessed with your mouth that Jesus is Lord and believed in your heart that God raised Him from the dead. God has given you power to become His child. You have eternal life!"

I want you to say, "I boldly confess that I am saved."

In Christ, we have the right to *know* that we are saved and to know that we have eternal life.

2. We Are Born Again in Christ

The second thing we have in Christ is the born-again experience. I want you to say, "*I am born again.*"

In John 3, Jesus was speaking to one of the most religious men of His day, Nicodemus, a devout Pharisee. He came to Jesus because religion did not and would never satisfy him.

If you ever wondered whether religion was enough to get a person to heaven, read these words of Jesus closely: "Jesus answered and said to him, 'Most assuredly, I say to you, unless one is born again, he cannot see the kingdom of God.' Nicodemus said to Him, 'How can a man be born when he is old? Can he enter a second time into his mother's womb and be born?' Jesus answered, 'Most assuredly, I say to you, unless one is born of water and the Spirit, he cannot enter the kingdom of God. That which is born of the flesh is flesh, and that which is born of the Spirit is spirit'" (John 3:3–6).

Thank God, *when we receive Jesus, we are born again.* "But as many as received Him, to them He gave the right to become children of God, to those who believe in His name: who were born, not of blood, nor of the will of the flesh, nor of the will of man, but of God" (John 1:12–13).

You are born of God! When you receive Jesus Christ as your Lord, you experience the new birth in your spirit. "Having been born again, not of corruptible seed but incorruptible, through the word of God which lives and abides forever" (1 Peter 1:23).

The new birth is like a natural birth in that you know there can be no birth without the implantation of a seed. Through the seed in a woman's body, our bodies were brought forth. The new birth takes place when a seed is planted in your spirit. That seed is the Word of God.

Nothing productive can take place in our lives until we have planted His Word inside us. The seed of God's Word in us is incorruptible, imperishable—it lives forever!

God's Word is the seed for every area of our lives, but we must take time to plant it inside of our spirit.

One day someone came along and planted a seed inside of you and me. They gave us the Gospel as Paul did to the Corinthians. "Moreover, brethren, I declare to you the gospel which I preached to you, which also

Nothing productive can take place in our lives until we have planted His Word inside us.

you received and in which you stand, by which also you are saved, if you hold fast that word which I preached to you—unless you believed in vain. For I delivered to you first of all that which I also received: that Christ died for our sins according to the Scriptures, and that He was buried, and that He rose again the third day according to the Scriptures" (1 Corinthians 15:1–4).

The Gospel consists of three facts:

1. Christ died for our sins.
2. He was buried.
3. He rose again.

Someone declared to us the Gospel. We believed it and united our faith with God's Word, that incorruptible seed, and inside of us a birth took place.

After I received Jesus, I looked just as I always did on the outside, but inside I was a new creature. You see, I was born again. I had a new kind of *life* inside, and I knew that I was born again. I had a desire to be with God's people and to read His Word. A change had taken place in me.

Make this bold declaration: *"I am saved. I am born again."*

Now, do not cast away your confidence. You may stumble and go back into the old life momentarily, but hold fast to your testimony. Say aloud, "I am miserable in this sin. Father, forgive me. Thank You, Lord, for cleansing me (see 1 John 1:9). Thank God, I know I am saved! I know I am born again."

When God saves us, He puts a light on the inside of us. "You are the light of the world. A city that is set on a hill cannot be hidden" (Matthew 5:14). I want you to say, *"I am the light of the world!"* because that is exactly what God says about you and me. He put a light on the inside of us, for He is "the Light of the world."

Some people have the idea that they are like a blinker light. They think they go on and off. Jesus does not go on and off in us. He keeps on shining even when we stumble and fall.

Many people wear themselves out, running from kingdom to kingdom. One moment they think they are in the kingdom of light; the next moment they think they are in the kingdom of darkness. They need to make a firm decision to believe God's Word. When we receive Jesus as our Lord and Savior, His light in us does not go out. We are indeed in the *kingdom of light.* The Light of lights dwells in us, and our light will never go out!

"Before anything else existed, there was Christ, with God. He has always been alive and is himself God. He created everything there is—nothing exists that he didn't make. Eternal life is in him, and this life gives light to all mankind. His life is the light that shines through the darkness—and the darkness can never extinguish it" (John 1:1–5 TLB).

3. We Are Made New Creatures in Christ

The third thing we have in Christ is a newly created spirit. I want you to say, "I am a new creature in Christ Jesus."

The Bible says we are saved, we are born again, and we are made new creatures. Inside your body, when you accepted Jesus, there burst into being a new creation. "Therefore, if anyone is in Christ, he is a new creation; old things have passed away; behold, all things have become new" (2 Corinthians 5:17).

Did you know that when you became a new creation, not only was your past forgiven, but your past also ceased to exist?

Have you ever held a newborn baby in your arms and said, "How wonderful—a new beginning!"? A newborn baby does not have a past.

The new creation in you has no past! Whether it is divorce, murder, immorality, perversion, or any other form of sin, *your past does not exist!* You are a newborn baby. You are a new creature. Old things are passed away and, behold, all things are become new. *You are a new creation!*

This new creation has the life of God—everlasting life. The moment you make the decision to believe on the Lord Jesus Christ, you are no longer condemned. "For God did not send His Son into the world to condemn the world, but that the world through Him might be saved. He who believes in Him is not condemned; but he who does not believe is condemned already, because he has not believed in the name of the only begotten Son of God" (John 3:17–18).

God assures us, "I, even I, am He who blots out your transgressions for My own sake; and *I will not remember your sins*" (Isaiah 43:25). Sins are wrong acts that are committed against an established law, even if the law is not known. He further assures us, "I have blotted out, like a thick cloud, your transgressions, and like a cloud, your sins" (Isaiah 44:22). Transgressions are wrong acts committed in open disobedience of a known law.

The prophet Isaiah compared sins and transgressions. Sins are as a cloud; transgressions are as a thick cloud. From Isaiah's comparison, we understand that transgressions are the darker of the two. Thank God, He not only cleared us of the past, but He made provision for us if we commit transgressions after we have come to know Christ as Savior. "If we confess our sins, He is faithful and just to forgive us our sins and to cleanse us from all unrighteousness" (1 John 1:9). If a believer sins and thereafter repents and confesses his sins, both he and the record of his life are completely cleansed.

If you are grieved when you sin, do not be sad. You should be happy because that is a sign that you are a new creature in Christ Jesus. "No one born (begotten) of God [deliberately, knowingly, and habitually] practices sin, for God's nature abides in him [His principle of life, the divine sperm, remains permanently within him]; and he cannot practice sinning because he is born (begotten) of God" (1 John 3:9 AMP).

Make this declaration: "I am a new creature in Christ Jesus. I am no longer condemned. God does not remember my sins. All my sins have been blotted out. If I sin, I will immediately confess my sins and be cleansed from all unrighteousness. Thank God, I have eternal life!"

4. We Are Delivered in Christ

The fourth thing we have in Christ is deliverance. I want you to say, "*I am delivered!*"

"Giving thanks to the Father who has qualified us to be partakers of the inheritance of the saints in the light. He has delivered us from the power of darkness and conveyed us into the kingdom of the Son of His love" (Colossians 1:12–13).

We are saved. We are born again. We are new creatures. We are delivered.

What have we been delivered from? We have been delivered from the power and the authority of darkness. You may be fighting old habits and struggling against old ways. Perhaps you do not know that you have the power *in you* to overcome these obstacles. I want to tell you that you have already been delivered!

Jesus said, "I am He who lives, and was dead, and behold, I am alive forevermore. Amen. And I have the keys of Hades and of Death" (Revelation 1:18). Boldly tell the enemy, "Jesus holds the keys to hell and to death, and no power of darkness can harm me or steal one day of my life. In the Name of Jesus, I command every power of darkness to flee (James 4:7)! I am delivered!"

God has already delivered you! You do not have to put up with those whirling thoughts of depression that come over you at times. You do not have to put up with those mental battles of discouragement and doubt. *Rise up* and boldly declare your deliverance!

You are not *going to be* delivered. You *are* delivered! You now walk in the kingdom of light. You have been translated into the kingdom of Jesus. "For you were once darkness, but now *you are* light in the Lord. Walk as children of light" (Ephesians 5:8).

Act like you are in the light. Declare your deliverance because you have it. Make this declaration: "I am delivered from the power of darkness. I am in the kingdom of light."

The moment you make the decision to believe

on the Lord Jesus Christ,

YOU ARE NO LONGER CONDEMNED.

5. WE ARE REDEEMED IN CHRIST

The fifth thing we have in Christ is redemption. I want you to say, "*I am redeemed.*"

"Christ has redeemed us from the curse of the law, having become a curse for us (for it is written, 'Cursed is everyone who hangs on a tree'), that the blessing of Abraham might come upon the Gentiles in Christ Jesus, that we might receive the promise of the Spirit through faith" (Galatians 3:13–14).

God states clearly that this redemption is based upon our response to His requirement: "But it shall come to pass, if you do not obey the voice of the LORD your God, to observe carefully all His commandments and His statutes which I command you today, that all these curses will come upon you and overtake you" (Deuteronomy 28:15).

God, through Jesus Christ, has given every man a choice. "I call heaven and earth as witnesses today against you, that I have set before you life and death, blessing and cursing; therefore choose life, that both you and your descendants may live; that you may love the LORD your God, that you may obey His voice, and that you may cling to Him, for He is your life and the length of your days" (Deuteronomy 30:19–20).

When we accept Jesus Christ as our Savior, we choose life, and we are redeemed. What are we redeemed from? We are redeemed from the curse of the law!

What does that mean? The Bible clearly defines the curse of the law in Deuteronomy 28:

- *Plagues*
- *Tumors*
- *Scabs*
- *Itch*
- *Madness*
- *Blindness*
- *Fever*
- *Poverty*
- *Darkness*
- *Powerless*
- *Oppression*
- *Adultery*
- *Despair*
- *Boils*
- *Captivity*
- *Idolatry*
- *Drought*
- *Mildew*
- *War*
- *Unburied*
- *Consumption*
- *Cursed in the city*
- *Cursed in the country*
- *Cursed in the basket*
- *Cursed in the bowl*
- *Children are cursed*
- *Produce is cursed*
- *Livestock is cursed*
- *Cursed when coming in*
- *Cursed when going out*
- *Confusion*
- *Rebuke*
- *Destruction*
- *Sow but not reap*
- *Will serve enemies*
- *Astonishment of heart*
- *Extreme burning*
- *You will be dispersed*
- *Enemies will defeat you*
- *Heaven shall be bronze*
- *Earth shall be iron*
- *Disappointment*

These are the grave consequences of disobedience. This is the misery of sin. But, thank God, we are redeemed from the curse of the law! "Oh, give thanks to the LORD, for He is good! For His mercy endures forever. Let the redeemed of the LORD *say* so, whom He has redeemed from the hand of the enemy" (Psalm 107:1–2).

David said, "Let the redeemed of the Lord *say* so." Say, "I am redeemed."

Look in the mirror and say these things. Say them to your spouse. "I am saved. I am born again. I am a new creature. I am delivered. I am redeemed." Say it so the enemy can hear you. Say it so the angels will rejoice with you!

"Knowing that you were not redeemed with corruptible things, like silver or gold, from your aimless conduct received by tradition from your fathers, but with the precious blood of Christ, as of a lamb without blemish and without spot" (1 Peter 1:18–19). *The price of our redemption is the precious blood of Jesus.* He spilled His blood on the cross of Calvary for every person.

The Bible says that Jesus became our High Priest and with His own precious blood He obtained eternal redemption for us. He ascended into heaven, and there, in the presence of the Father, He presented His blood so that we could have forgiveness of sins (Hebrews 9:11–13; 12:22–24).

The blood of Jesus Christ is ever before the Father as evidence that we have been redeemed from every oppressive curse and every wicked work of the enemy. "In Him we have redemption through His blood, the forgiveness of sins, according to the riches of His grace" (Ephesians 1:7). Through the blood of Jesus, *we are redeemed!*

In the Old Testament, God instructed the children of Israel to kill a lamb and put the blood on their doorposts. This is known as the Passover, and it protected them from the death angel. "Now the blood shall be a sign for you on the houses where you are. And when I see the blood, I will pass over you; and the plague shall not be on you to destroy you when I strike the land of Egypt" (Exodus 12:13).

In the New Testament, Jesus celebrated the Passover with His disciples. He took the cup and spoke these words: "For this is My blood of the new covenant, which is shed for many for the remission of sins. But I say to you, I will not drink of this fruit of the vine from now on until that day when I drink it new with you in My Father's kingdom" (Matthew 26:28–29).

Jesus Himself was offered for the sins of the world. His blood was shed for our sins—He paid the price. But the responsibility of applying the blood of Jesus to the doorposts of our lives rests upon us. "Seeing then that we have a great High Priest who has passed through the heavens, Jesus the Son of God, let us hold fast our confession" (Hebrews 4:14).

By our confession, we testify to Satan and all powers of darkness what the Word of God says the blood of Jesus does for us! "And they overcame him by the blood of the Lamb and by the word of their testimony, and they did not love their lives to the death" (Revelation 12:11).

God is looking for blood on the doorposts of our lives. Where He does not find the blood of Jesus, there is no protection. He is not interested in which church we attend—He simply requires that we accept His Son as Savior.

THE BLOOD OF JESUS CHRIST IS EVER BEFORE

the Father as evidence that we have been

redeemed from every oppressive curse

and every wicked work of the enemy.

When the enemy brings temptations into your life, remind him of the blood that bought your redemption. Say boldly: "Through the blood of Jesus, I am redeemed! I am redeemed from the curse of the law!"

6. We Are Blessed in Christ

The sixth thing we have in Christ is the blessing of Abraham. I want you to say, *"I am blessed."*

"Christ has redeemed us from the curse of the law, having become a curse for us (for it is written, 'Cursed is everyone who hangs on a tree'), that the blessing of Abraham might come upon the Gentiles in Christ Jesus, that we might receive the promise of the Spirit through faith" (Galatians 3:13–14).

I want you to say: "I am saved. I am born again. I am a new creature. I am delivered. I am redeemed. I am blessed."

"Now it shall come to pass, if you diligently obey the voice of the Lord your God, to observe carefully all His commandments which I command you today, that the Lord your God will set you high above all nations of the earth. And all these blessings shall come upon you and overtake you, because you obey the voice of the Lord your God" (Deuteronomy 28:1–2).

In Deuteronomy 28, we find the blessing of Abraham:

- *Blessed in the city*
- *Blessed in the country*
- *Children will be blessed*
- *Land will be blessed*
- *Livestock will be blessed*
- *Basket will be blessed*
- *Blessed coming in*
- *Blessed going out*
- *Enemies will flee before you seven ways*
- *Blessed in storehouses*
- *Blessed in all you put your hand to*
- *Established as a holy people*
- *People can see that you are called by the Name of the Lord*
- *People of the earth will be afraid of you*
- *Surplus of prosperity through the fruit of your body, livestock, and ground*
- *The Lord will give rain to your land*
- *The Lord will bless all the work of your hand*
- *You will lend and not borrow*
- *You will be the head and not the tail*
- *You will be above only and not beneath*

If you study Abraham's life, you will find that it was never recorded that he was sick. His wife was so beautiful at ninety years of age that another man wanted her. The Bible says, "Abram was very rich in livestock, in silver, and in gold" (Genesis 13:2).

If you are in a financial crisis, read the first fourteen verses of Deuteronomy 28 and remember that *Christ has redeemed you from the curse of the law in order that the blessing of Abraham might come on you through Jesus Christ.*

Let your eyes rest on the blessing of Abraham, as you meditate day and night on these promises of God:

- *Your financial situation will turn around.*
- *Your land will be blessed.*
- *Your children will be blessed.*
- *Your cattle will be blessed.*
- *Your enemies will flee from you.*
- *You will be known as a holy people.*
- *Your business will be blessed.*

Begin to partake of these great blessings that God has provided for you and your family.

7. We Are Overcomers in Christ

The seventh thing we have in Christ is the ability to be an overcomer. I want you to say, "*I have overcome.*"

"You are of God, little children, and have overcome them, because He who is in you is greater than he who is in the world" (1 John 4:4).

What does it mean to overcome? It means *to win the victory over.* You may say, "Now, just a minute. There is no way I can have victory in my situation."

Yes, you can! Reread 1 John 4:4 and begin to meditate on what God said through the apostle John. Because God is in you, you have overcome.

Have you paused long enough today to remember that you are not in the battle alone? God dwells in you. "Do you not know that you are the temple of God and that the Spirit of God dwells in you?" (1 Corinthians 3:16).

We are of God—we are not of this world. We are in the world, but we are not of the world. We do not belong to this world.

Do not remain a child in your Christian life. Begin to understand how you have been blessed. "Now I say that the heir, as long as he is a child, does not differ at all from a slave, though he is master of all" (Galatians 4:1).

God, through Jesus Christ, has brought total victory in every area of our lives, but we must enforce that victory. When you open your heart and receive these great truths, you can overcome sickness, depression, fear, torment, and every other curse of the law.

God predestined us to be *victorious* over:

- Evil influences of men—*"Through You we will push down our enemies; through Your name we will trample those who rise up against us" (Psalm 44:5).*

- Powers of darkness—*"Behold, I give you the authority to trample on serpents and scorpions, and over all the power of the enemy, and nothing shall by any means hurt you" (Luke 10:19).*

- Circumstances of life—*"Who shall separate us from the love of Christ? Shall tribulation, or distress, or persecution, or famine, or nakedness, or peril, or sword? Yet in all these things we are more than conquerors through Him who loved us" (Romans 8:35, 37). "Now thanks be to God who always leads us in triumph in Christ, and through us diffuses the fragrance of His knowledge in every place" (2 Corinthians 2:14).*

- Worldly attractions—*"For whatever is born of God overcomes the world. And this is the victory that has overcome the world—our faith"* (1 John 5:4).
- Satanic power at the end of the age— *"And I saw something like a sea of glass mingled with fire, and those who have the victory over the beast, over his image and over his mark and over the number of his name, standing on the sea of glass, having harps of God"* (Revelation 15:2).

You may be in a battle today for your life, but you can overcome! Take the Word of God and the blood of Jesus and defeat the enemy. You can do it because greater is He that is in you than he that is in the world! "And they overcame [Satan] by the blood of the Lamb and by the word of their testimony, and they did not love their lives to the death" (Revelation 12:11).

Let us imagine that we are at the throne of God. Jesus—His beloved Son who bears the marks of Calvary—is at His right hand. He loves us with an everlasting love. He is God manifested in the flesh, the visible representation of the invisible God. Angels are lingering near. Satan, the accuser of the brethren, has come to accuse us. In the presence of Jesus, we want to tell the Father something. We want to say, "We are saved. We are born again. We are new creatures. We are delivered. We are redeemed. We are blessed. We are overcomers."

Now I want you to say it just for yourself. "I am saved. I am born again. I am a new creature. I am delivered. I am redeemed. I am blessed. I have overcome!"

The Father smiles, Jesus rejoices, angels dance for you, and Satan trembles!

GOD, THROUGH JESUS CHRIST,

has brought total victory in every area of our lives,

but we must enforce that victory.

Reflections from
JOEL

There was a man who traveled across the Atlantic on a cruise ship but never ate in the dining room. Instead, he would go off in a corner and eat cheese and crackers he had brought with him. Near the end of the trip, another man asked him, "Why don't you come into the banquet hall and eat with us?" The traveler's face flushed with embarrassment. "Well, to tell you the truth, I had only enough money to buy the ticket." The other passenger shook his head and said, "Sir, the meals were included in the price of the ticket!"

Many of us are missing out on God's best because we don't realize that the good things in life have already been paid for in our redemption (1 Corinthians 7:23). We are surviving on cheese and crackers, while God has made much more available to us in Christ.

CHAPTER SIX

A Declaration

of

Deliverance

T oday, whether they recognize the source or not, many people are oppressed by Satan and the powers of darkness. They are miserable and tormented by guilt and doubt and lies. While many believers seem to be completely unaware that they are being assaulted by the powers of darkness, there are others who talk of demons and their work constantly. Neither is valid or profitable.

Let your eyes rest on the scriptures listed on the following pages. Let your mind dwell on the eternal truths set forth in these verses. Meditate on them. They helped me, and they will help you.

Boldly take the Word of God and train yourself to make it your constant confession. Read these scriptures aloud. Deliberately come before the throne of God with His Word and with this confession, and the enemy must flee from you!

Remember, what you continue to believe in your heart and say with your mouth will come to pass in your life. Never allow your mouth to speak what is contrary to God's Word.

What the Word of God Says About You

- *"Let us therefore come boldly to the throne of grace, that we may obtain mercy and find grace to help in time of need"* (Hebrews 4:16).
- *"Therefore, holy brethren, partakers of the heavenly calling, consider the Apostle and High Priest of our confession, Christ Jesus"* (Hebrews 3:1).
- *"Take words with you, and return to the Lord. Say to Him, 'Take away all iniquity; receive us graciously, for we will offer the sacrifices of our lips'"* (Hosea 14:2).
- *"Now this is the confidence that we have in Him, that if we ask anything according to His will, He hears us. And if we know that He hears us, whatever we ask, we know that we have the petitions that we have asked of Him"* (1 John 5:14–15).
- *"Death and life are in the power of the tongue, and those who love it will eat its fruit"* (Proverbs 18:21).

- "For assuredly, I say to you, whoever says to this mountain, 'Be removed and be cast into the sea,' and does not doubt in his heart, but believes that those things he says will be done, he will have whatever he says" (Mark 11:23).

- "He has delivered us from the power of darkness and conveyed us into the kingdom of the Son of His love" (Colossians 1:13).

- "And you He made alive, who were dead in trespasses and sins, in which you once walked according to the course of this world, according to the prince of the power of the air, the spirit who now works in the sons of disobedience" (Ephesians 2:1–2).

- "Nor give place to the devil" (Ephesians 4:27).

- "For the kingdom of God is not eating and drinking, but righteousness and peace and joy in the Holy Spirit" (Romans 14:17).

- "But seek first the kingdom of God and His righteousness, and all these things shall be added to you" (Matthew 6:33).

- "Behold, I give you the authority to trample on serpents and scorpions, and over all the power of the enemy, and nothing shall by any means hurt you" (Luke 10:19).

- *"And these signs will follow those who believe: In My name they will cast out demons; they will speak with new tongues" (Mark 16:17).*
- *"Therefore submit to God. Resist the devil and he will flee from you" (James 4:7).*
- *"And they overcame him by the blood of the Lamb and by the word of their testimony, and they did not love their lives to the death" (Revelation 12:11).*
- *"He who sins is of the devil, for the devil has sinned from the beginning. For this purpose the Son of God was manifested, that He might destroy the works of the devil" (1 John 3:8).*
- *"Having disarmed principalities and powers, He made a public spectacle of them, triumphing over them in it" (Colossians 2:15).*
- *"Or how can one enter a strong man's house and plunder his goods, unless he first binds the strong man? And then he will plunder his house" (Matthew 12:29).*
- *"Yet in all these things we are more than conquerors through Him who loved us" (Romans 8:37).*
- *"This is the day the LORD has made; we will rejoice and be glad in it" (Psalm 118:24).*

A PERSONAL DECLARATION OF DELIVERANCE

"Father, as I approach Your throne now with my declaration, Your Word says, 'Let us therefore come boldly to the throne of grace, that we may obtain mercy and find grace to help in time of need' (Hebrews 4:16). As I come to boldly confess, I realize that Jesus is the High Priest of my confession (see Hebrews 3:1). You said, 'Take words with you, and return to the LORD' (Hosea 14:2).

"Father, I come to Your throne in the face of all the doubt . . . in the face of all the assaults of the enemy . . . in the face of all the forces of darkness . . . *to boldly confess Your Word!*

"Lord, I know that You listen to me when I pray and speak to You according to Your Word. The Word of God says that if we ask anything according to Your will (Your Word), You hear us. And if You hear us, we know we have the petitions we ask of You (see 1 John 5:14–15).

"Father, I know that my confession is important because death and life are in the power of the tongue (Proverbs 18:21).

"Lord, You said in Your Word that I could have whatever I say (see Mark 11:23). I boldly confess Your Word concerning myself as a new creature in Christ Jesus. I come with that Word in my mouth, believing it in my heart.

"I boldly declare before You, Father, before the Lord Jesus Christ, and before the powers of darkness: *I am born again! I am redeemed! I am delivered!*

"Father, I want to dwell upon Your Word that says I am delivered from the power of darkness and translated into the kingdom of Your dear Son (see Colossians 1:13). I thank You that I am not going to be delivered, *but I am delivered!*

"Your Word teaches that there are two kingdoms—a kingdom of light and a kingdom of darkness. In the kingdom of darkness, Satan is lord, and there is misery, doubt, unforgiveness of sins, sickness, oppression, deep depression, and mental anguish. There are demonic forces that harass and vex the members of that kingdom. When I was lost, '[I] once walked according to the course of this world, according to the prince of the power of the air, the spirit who now works in the sons of disobedience' (Ephesians 2:2). I walked in that darkness and was so unhappy. I did not have the joy of the Lord or eternal life.

"But, Father, I thank You that one day the Lord Jesus became my Lord and my Savior and called me into fellowship with Him. By Your grace and mercy, You revealed Jesus to me, and I made Him my Lord. When I made Jesus my Lord, I was delivered from the powers of darkness and translated into the kingdom of Your dear Son!

"Father, I want to remind You that *I have been delivered!* I want to remind the Lord Jesus Christ and the holy angels of God! Satan, I remind you and all the demon forces that follow you that *I have been delivered* by the power of Jesus Christ, by His Name and by His blood! I am delivered from the power of darkness, and I have been translated into the kingdom of light! You have no authority or power over me, Satan.

"The Bible says, 'Nor give place to the devil' (Ephesians 4:27). Satan, I have given you a place in my life at times, but I will not do it anymore. You have no authority or power over me whatsoever! I have been delivered from all of your power. Satan, I command you, *in the Name of the Lord Jesus Christ,* to leave me now!

"Father, I rejoice that the enemy has no legal or spiritual authority over me whatsoever. I am walking and living in the kingdom of light—the kingdom of Your Son. Lord, Your kingdom is not sickness, depression, evil and wickedness, oppression, vexation, trouble, and sorrow. I walk in the kingdom of God, which is 'righteousness and peace and joy in the Holy Spirit' (Romans 14:17). I praise You, Lord!

"Jesus, You said, 'But seek first the kingdom of God and His righteousness, and all these things shall be added to you' (Matthew 6:33). Father, I seek *first* Your kingdom today. I know that as I am obedient to Your Word, all the problems and all the things I have before me will be taken care of. That is Your business. My business is to seek first the kingdom of God, and as I do, my family will be taken care of, my business will prosper, and my prayers will be answered.

"I rejoice that You said in Your Word, 'Behold, I give you the authority to trample on serpents and scorpions, and over all the power of the enemy, and nothing shall by any means hurt you' (Luke 10:19). Oh, Father, I confess boldly with my mouth: I have power over all the power of the enemy, and nothing shall by any means hurt me.

"It is almost too big for me to understand, and yet I accept in my spirit that I have power in the Name of the Lord Jesus Christ and by the power of His blood—not over one demon, one hundred demons, or one thousand demons, but over every demonic force, all the demon forces combined, and over Satan himself! You have given me power over all the power of the enemy and nothing shall by any means hurt me—not what I have done in the past (which has ceased to exist), not what I face now, or what I shall face in the future!

"Your Word says, 'In My name they will cast out demons' (Mark 16:17). The Bible also says, 'Therefore submit to God. Resist the devil and he will flee from you' (James 4:7). In the light of God's Word, I come against every

My business is to seek first the kingdom of God, and as I do, my family will be taken care of, my business will prosper, and my prayers will be answered.

power of darkness that is arrayed against me, my family, my business, and everything I am involved in. *I command you, Satan, to leave* me, my family, all those for whom I am praying, and those in my circle of influence in the Name of Jesus!

"I command you to take your hands off my business! I command you to take your hands off my children! I command you, *in the Name of Jesus Christ,* to take your hands off my spirit, mind, body, and all that I have to do today. Flee from me, Satan, according to the Word of God!

"*Jesus is my Lord!* In the Name of the Lord Jesus Christ, I have dispelled and caused to flee from me every demonic force! I am thankful that the Word of God says, 'And they overcame him by the blood of the Lamb and by the word of their testimony, and they did not love their lives to the death' (Revelation 12:11). By my confession of the Word of God, I hold up the blood of the Lord Jesus Christ.

"Satan, I boldly declare to you that the blood of Jesus is my shield and the Word of God is my testimony. Do not dare come near me or my household. You are a defeated foe. Your works have been destroyed. Jesus spoiled principalities and powers. He made a show of them openly, triumphing over them in the cross (see Colossians 2:15). Satan, you are spoiled and a defeated foe!

"Jesus said, 'Or how can one enter a strong man's house and plunder his goods, unless he first binds the strong man? And then he will plunder his house' (Matthew 12:29). Jesus has already entered your house, Satan! He has taken from you all of your armor. He has spoiled your goods and divided His victory with me! He has shared His victory with every child of God!

"Oh, Father, I thank You that I have been translated into the kingdom of God's dear Son! I am not going to be, I am! Lord, I thank You that in this kingdom of light there is righteousness, peace, and joy in the Holy Spirit. I rejoice because You are my Father, Jesus Christ is my Lord and Savior, and the Holy Spirit dwells within my body. I am more than a conqueror through Him who loves me. I have no fear, for I have been delivered from the power of darkness. I rejoice and bless the Name of the Lord. This is the day the Lord has made. I choose to rejoice and be glad in it!

"I have been delivered from Satan's power!"

Reflections from
JOEL

What mountain is in front of you—a sickness, a troubled relationship, a floundering business? Jesus said, "For assuredly, I say to you, whoever says to this mountain, 'Be removed and be cast into the sea,' and does not doubt in his heart, but believes that those things he says will be done, he will have whatever he says." Whatever your mountain is, you must do more than think or pray about it; you must speak to that obstacle.

The Bible says, "Let the weak say, 'I am strong'" (Joel 3:10). Start calling yourself healed, happy, whole, blessed, and prosperous. God is a miracle-working God. Stop talking to God about how big your mountains are, and starting talking to your mountains about how big your God is!

CHAPTER SEVEN

A Declaration *of* Strength *to* Overcome

The Word of God is alive, and it is the sword of the Spirit. The Word of God, spoken out of our mouths, will defeat the enemy!

Your enemy, Satan, is carefully organized. His purpose is to steal, kill, and destroy all that you hold dear. But do not be afraid of the enemy!

God encourages us in His Word to be strong and very courageous. Read the Word of God, and speak the Word of God. It will penetrate the darkness around you. By speaking the Word of God, you will rise above any obstacle and walk in the victory that God has prepared for you.

What the Word of God Says About You

- *"Finally, my brethren, be strong in the Lord and in the power of His might. Put on the whole armor of God, that you may be able to stand against the wiles of the devil. For we do not wrestle against flesh and blood, but against principalities, against powers, against the rulers of the darkness of this age, against spiritual hosts of wickedness in the heavenly places. Therefore take up the whole armor of God, that you may be able to withstand in the evil day, and having done all, to stand. Stand therefore, having girded your waist with truth, having put on the breastplate of righteousness, and having shod your feet with the preparation of the gospel of peace; above all, taking the shield of faith with which you will be able to quench all the fiery darts of the wicked one. And take the helmet of salvation, and the sword of the Spirit, which is the word of God; praying always with all prayer and supplication in the Spirit, being watchful to this end with all perseverance and supplication for all the saints"* (Ephesians 6:10–18).
- *"For assuredly, I say to you, whoever says to this mountain, 'Be removed and be cast into the sea,' and does not doubt in his heart, but believes that those things he says will be done, he will have whatever he says"* (Mark 11:23).

- *"Death and life are in the power of the tongue, and those who love it will eat its fruit" (Proverbs 18:21).*
- *"Beat your plowshares into swords and your pruning hooks into spears; let the weak say, 'I am strong'" (Joel 3:10).*
- *"I have written to you, fathers, because you have known Him who is from the beginning. I have written to you, young men, because you are strong, and the word of God abides in you, and you have overcome the wicked one" (1 John 2:14).*
- *"For this reason I bow my knees to the Father of our Lord Jesus Christ, from whom the whole family in heaven and earth is named, that He would grant you, according to the riches of His glory, to be strengthened with might through His Spirit in the inner man" (Ephesians 3:14–16).*
- *"The LORD is my light and my salvation; whom shall I fear? The LORD is the strength of my life; of whom shall I be afraid?" (Psalm 27:1).*
- *"Therefore, if anyone is in Christ, he is a new creation; old things have passed away; behold, all things have become new" (2 Corinthians 5:17).*
- *"The thief does not come except to steal, and to kill, and to destroy. I have come that they may have life, and that they may have it more abundantly" (John 10:10).*

- *"For the weapons of our warfare are not carnal but mighty in God for pulling down strongholds, casting down arguments and every high thing that exalts itself against the knowledge of God, bringing every thought into captivity to the obedience of Christ"* (2 Corinthians 10:4–5).

A Personal Declaration of Victorious Strength

"Father, I come to make my declaration of Your Word before Your great throne of mercy. You are my Father. Jesus, You are my Lord and Savior. The Holy Spirit dwells within my body, and I am covered with the blood of the Lord Jesus Christ. The angels of God attend my way.

"Lord, I do not believe all that my eyes see, all that my body feels, and all that the enemy would bring against me. I know that I shall rise no higher nor sink lower than my confession.

"I dare to boldly speak Your Word! And as I confess Your Word, my body will line up with Your Word, my mind will obey Your Word, and my spirit will rise to the level of Your Word.

"I thank You that You have placed a law within us and within Your Word. We shall have whatever we say, and the power of life and death is in the tongue (see Mark 11:23

and Proverbs 18:21). Lord, I choose life! Life is mine—not death.

"Father, I come to boldly declare that I am strong—spiritually, mentally, emotionally, physically, financially, and materially. I thank You that I am strong in my body, mind, and spirit. *I am strong!*

"Lord, the Bible says, 'Let the weak say, "I *am* strong"' (Joel 3:10). It does not say, 'Let the weak pray.' It says, 'Let the weak *say*, "I am strong."' Therefore I say *I am strong!*

"Father, I boldly come to Your throne of grace and make my confession according to Your Word. I am strong because the Word of God abides within me. I am strengthened with all might by Your Spirit in the inner man. I am strong because the Lord is my light and my salvation—whom shall I fear? The Lord is the strength of my life, of whom shall I be afraid? (see Psalm 27:1).

"The scriptures that I have before me are true. I stand before Your throne and boldly declare out of my mouth, believing in my heart that these words are true. 'Finally, my brethren, be strong in the Lord and in the power of His might' (Ephesians 6:10). It does not matter what my body or my mind or what my circumstances may say. Lord, I declare that I am strong in You and in the power of Your might. First of all, Father, I want to thank You that I am in the Lord. *I am in Jesus,* and 'if anyone is in

Christ, he is a new creation' (2 Corinthians 5:17). I am in Christ. I have redemption and all the blessings of God.

"Father, I put on Your whole armor, and I am able to stand against *all* the wiles and strategies of the enemy. I know that Satan comes against me in every form and fashion, lying, stealing, and trying to destroy. But Jesus declared, 'I have come that they may have life, and that they may have it more abundantly' (John 10:10).

"Father, I know that anything that steals, kills, or destroys is not of You. I thank You, Father, that I am able to stand against all the wiles of the devil. I know that I wrestle not against flesh and blood. I wrestle against principalities, powers, the rulers of the darkness of this world, and wicked spirits in high places.

"Because of these wicked, evil spirits and demonic forces, I have taken unto me the whole armor of God. I am able to withstand in this evil day, and having done all and overcome all, *I stand!* Father, there is *no* fear in my heart or in my mind. I am an overcomer because I believe that Jesus Christ is the Son of God.

"I stand, therefore, having my waist girded about with truth. I have on the breastplate of righteousness. My feet are shod with the preparation of the gospel of peace. Above all, I have taken the shield of faith wherewith I quench all the fiery darts of the wicked. I have on the helmet of salvation, and I take the sword of the Spirit, which is the Word of God. I am praying always with all prayer and supplication in the Spirit and watching thereunto with all perseverance for all saints.

"Father, I thank You that I am dressed for battle. I am a soldier of the Lord Jesus Christ. The Bible says, 'You therefore must endure hardship as a good soldier of Jesus Christ' (2 Timothy 2:3).

"I take the Word of God, and I boldly declare that I have on God's armor and I am strong. I have all power over all the power of the enemy, and nothing shall by any means hurt me!

"Lord, I thank You that the weapons of my warfare are not carnal, but mighty through God to the pulling down of strongholds, casting down imaginations, and bringing every thought into the captivity of Christ (see 2 Corinthians 10:4–5).

"I have the blood of Jesus Christ and the Name of Jesus Christ. I have the nature of God and the Holy Spirit in my life. I rejoice and bless the Name of the Lord God that I am more than a conqueror through Him who loved me. I am not only a conqueror, but *more* than a conqueror through Him who loved me! I can do all things through Christ who strengthens me!

"*I am strong!* I am strong in my spirit, my body, and my mind. I am strong financially. I am strong to do mighty exploits for God. I boldly confess before all I meet today that I am strong! Father, I rejoice in Your strength. I am strong in You, Lord, and in the power of Your might!

"Therefore, I banish every fear. I command weakness to leave me in all areas because it does not belong. It is the curse of the law, and it has nothing to do with me. I confess it with my mouth. Father, Your Word says that I can have whatever I say. I believe it right now, whether I feel it or not. I am strong in every area of my life. I rejoice in You, Lord, and in the power of Your might that exists in my body!

"Father, I stand before You unafraid. I rejoice! I praise You! I thank You with all my heart that *my confession* becomes *my possession.* I am strong in the Lord and in the power of His might!

"*I have strength to overcome every attack of Satan, every trial, and every obstacle in my way.*"

By speaking the Word of God, you will rise above any obstacle and walk in the victory that God has prepared for you.

Reflections from
JOEL

I heard about a doctor who understood the power of words. One prescription he gave to all his patients was for them to say at least once every hour, "I'm getting better and better every day, in every way." His patients experienced amazing results, much better than the patients treated by many of his colleagues.

When you say something often enough, with enthusiasm and passion, before long your subconscious mind begins to act on what you are saying, doing whatever is necessary to bring those thoughts and words to pass. If you struggle with low self-esteem, go overboard in speaking words of victory about your life. Get up each morning and say, "I am valuable and loved. God has a great plan for my life. I'm excited about my future." There truly is power in your words.

CHAPTER EIGHT

A Declaration

of

Prosperity

and Victory

N othing has given me more delight than declaring the Psalms before the Lord.

This confession is based on Psalm 1. Read this wonderful psalm right now. Meditate upon it, and let it sink into your spirit.

Once it is fresh in your heart, lift up your voice and make the following declaration before the Lord. Make your confession several times daily. As you continually speak the Word of God, it will become your own. The truth of God's Word will sink into your heart, and your lips will begin to speak it out with great assurance.

Blessed is the man
  Who walks not in the counsel of the ungodly,
  Nor stands in the path of sinners,
  Nor sits in the seat of the scornful;
But his delight is in the law of the LORD,
  And in His law he meditates day and night.
He shall be like a tree
  Planted by the rivers of water,
  That brings forth its fruit in its season,
  Whose leaf also shall not wither;
  And whatever he does shall prosper.

PSALM 1:1–3

A PERSONAL DECLARATION OF PROSPERITY AND VICTORY

"Father, I come before You with Your Word in my heart and upon my lips. I know the Bible says, 'For assuredly, I say to you, whoever says to this mountain, "Be removed and be cast into the sea," and does not doubt in his heart, but believes that those things he says will be done, he will have whatever he says' (Mark 11:23).

"I will not say that I am defeated and weak or that I am down or that I have trouble and sorrow. I will not say that I cannot do the things that I have to do.

"Lord, I will say what Your Word says. I dare to come before Your throne boldly, knowing that the Lord Jesus Christ is the High Priest of my confession.

"I put Your words in my mouth because I believe that Your Word is eternally settled in heaven (see Psalm 119:89). It is settled in my heart! I believe that Your Word is alive and powerful and sharper than any two-edged sword (see Hebrews 4:12). Lord, I believe that Your Word will never return to You void, but it shall prosper in the thing for which You sent it (see Isaiah 55:11).

"Today, Lord, I take this blessed psalm, and I bring it to You. I make this psalm my own, for it is the eternal Word of God. Therefore, I say, I am not cursed—I am blessed. I am not sad—I am happy. I am not filled with depression—I am filled with joy. I say that I am blessed. I am blessed in my home. I am blessed because I have health and strength. I am blessed, O Lord God, because I have Your promises.

"I am blessed because I walk not in the counsel of the ungodly. I stand not in the path of sinners, and I sit not in the seat of the scornful.

"I boldly confess that *I will counsel with godly people.* Your Word is my counselor. The Holy Spirit is my counselor, and the Lord Jesus is my counselor.

"I boldly confess that *I will not stand in the path of sinners.* I will not go to the places where sin abounds. I will not talk like sinners. I will not live like sinners. I am redeemed—I am a child of God.

"I boldly confess that *I will not sit in the seat of the scornful.* I will not be filled with unforgiveness, jealousy, or pride. I will not be filled with hatred or ill feelings. I will not be scornful toward life.

"I boldly declare that my delight is in the law of the Lord. My delight is not to do evil or to walk in the way of the world. My delight is not to fill my heart and mind with the things of this world. My delight is in the law of the Lord!

"Lord, I take the great promises and truths of the Word of God, and I meditate upon them day and night. As I begin the day, drive to work, and go about the duties of the day, I meditate upon Your Word. When trouble arises, Lord, Your Word is within my heart. Even when I lie down at night, I meditate upon the great promises of God. 'Let the words of my mouth and

I am more than a conqueror through Him who loved me. I am not only a conqueror, but more than a conqueror through Him who loved me!

the meditation of my heart be acceptable in Your sight, O LORD, my strength and my Redeemer' (Psalm 19:14).

"Lord, because I meditate upon Your Word both day and night, I am like a tree planted by the rivers of water. My roots go down deep, Lord God, and reach the sustenance and the power of the water of Life that the world does not know anything about. I bring forth my fruit in its season. Lord, I declare that I am bringing forth fruit. I am a blessing to people today. I am winning souls and helping and encouraging people. I am bringing forth fruit in my daily life.

"My leaf also shall not wither. Lord God, nothing in my life shall wither. I will not live a withered life. My life is filled with life and strength and the power of the Holy Spirit.

MY BUSINESS IS TO SEEK FIRST

THE KINGDOM OF GOD,

and as I do, my family will be taken care of,

my business will prosper,

and my prayers will be answered.

"I boldly declare that whatever I do shall prosper. I am not a failure. I boldly declare that I am not cast down in defeat, but whatever I do shall prosper. It does not matter what circumstances may look like. Lord God, I confess what Your Word says. I am prospering— spiritually, physically, mentally, and financially. I am prospering in my marriage and in every area of my life. I am prospering because of the Word of the living God. Whatever I do shall prosper!

"Lord, I praise You that this is true. I boldly declare, confirm, and confess that You are with me and that You will never leave me nor forsake me. Just as You were with Moses, Joshua, Elijah, and the Lord Jesus Christ— *I declare that You are with me.*

"Lord, You commanded Joshua to be strong and of good courage. I like to meditate on the words You spoke to him because I know that You are speaking to me, also. 'Only be strong and very courageous, that you may observe to do according to all the law which Moses My servant commanded you; do not turn from it to the right hand or to the left, that you may prosper wherever you go' (Joshua 1:7).

"Lord, this is my confession: I am strong and of good courage. I observe to do Your law, the *law of love*. I will live in love and obey your commandments, Lord. I will obey Your law, and I will not turn from it to the right hand or to the left. I will prosper wherever I go.

"I boldly declare, according to Joshua 1:8, 'This Book of the Law shall not depart from [my] mouth, but [I] shall meditate in it day and night.' I thank You that whatever I do will prosper and wherever I go I will prosper.

"Lord, have You not commanded me to be strong and of good courage? I am not afraid or dismayed! I am not afraid of life or death. I am not afraid of problems, circumstances, or people. I am not afraid of the powers of darkness. I am not afraid of anything I face. I am not dismayed or discouraged. *Why?* Because, Lord God, You are with me wherever I go. You are the strength of my life.

"I am blessed. Today I will rejoice and be a blessing to all I meet. I boldly make this confession. I believe it in my heart and confess it with my mouth. It is mine. It materializes because You, Lord, said that I can have whatever I say.

"I boldly declare that as I meet people and they ask me how I am, I will say, 'I am blessed!' I will have a good report for all I meet. I will not talk of sickness and weakness and problems. I will talk as though You were with me, because You are with me. I will let those I meet hear the joyful sound from my lips: *'I am blessed of the Lord my God!'* Father, I rejoice because these words are eternally true and they are mine.

"*I am living in prosperity and victory!*"

TODAY I WILL REJOICE

and be a blessing to all I meet.

Reflections from
JOEL

God has not given us hundreds of promises in His Word simply for us to read. God has given us His promises so we might boldly declare them to bring us victory, health, hope, and abundant life. The Scripture says, "With the heart one believes unto righteousness, and with the mouth confession is made unto salvation" (Romans 10:10). When you believe God's Word and begin to speak it, mixing it with faith, you are actually confirming that truth and making it valid in your own life.

If you are facing sickness or struggling financially, boldly declare what the Word of God has to say about it. Friend, when you make those kinds of bold declarations, God will work to accomplish all that His Word says.

CHAPTER NINE

A Declaration *of* God's Abundant Supply

Good wants to meet our needs. His desire is that we be at peace with Him and with ourselves. He wants us to be totally free from worry and fear.

Psalm 23 is a beautiful expression of God's love for us. Meditate on these scriptures until you know in your spirit that God will take care of you and supply all of your needs.

Make the following declaration with a thankful heart. Learn to praise and worship God because of His love for you.

The LORD is my shepherd;
>I shall not want.
He makes me to lie down in green pastures;
>He leads me beside the still waters.
He restores my soul;
>He leads me in the paths of righteousness
>For His name's sake.
Yea, though I walk through the valley
>>of the shadow of death,
>I will fear no evil;
>For You are with me;
>Your rod and Your staff, they comfort me.
You prepare a table before me in the presence
>>of my enemies;
>You anoint my head with oil;
>My cup runs over.
Surely goodness and mercy shall follow me
>All the days of my life;
>And I will dwell in the house of the LORD
>Forever.

PSALM 23

A PERSONAL DECLARATION OF GOD'S ABUNDANT SUPPLY

"Father, I rejoice because I am Your child and You are my Father. I rejoice because Jesus is seated at Your right hand, ever living to make intercession for me.

"Your Word says to come boldly to the throne of grace in order to obtain mercy and find grace to help in the time of need. Lord, You know every need I have in my spirit, mind, and physical body. You know every need I have materially and financially. You know every need I have in my family circle. You know every heartache and every burden that I bear.

"Lord, according to Your Word, I know that I shall have whatever I say. Many times the things that I have said—my wrong confessions—have brought destruction in my life. But I have found a truth: *If I will change what I say and confess Your Word, I can change what I have.*

"I will not confess what my body feels, what my eyes see, or what my senses tell me, but I will boldly speak Your Word, knowing that I shall have whatever I say.

"I take Psalm 23 and make it my own. I confess it at Your throne. Lord Jesus, You are my Shepherd. You said, 'I am the good shepherd' (John 10:14). The good shepherd gives His life for the sheep. I thank You because You are *my* Shepherd and the Shepherd of the great family of God.

"Lord, You are the One who feeds me, guides me, and shields me. I boldly confess that You are my Shepherd who watches over me when the world forgets me. There is One I know who looks down upon me. Your eyes never fail to follow me. Your love surrounds me because You love me so dearly. You will not fail me or my family!

"Because You are my Shepherd, Lord Jesus, I boldly say, *I do not want!* I do not lack. I do not have a care or any anxiety. I do not have one burden, because I cast my burden upon the Lord. I bless Your Holy Name! Lord, You sustain me.

"I do not want, Lord, because You are supplying every need that I have. Has not Your Word said, 'And my God shall supply all your need according to His riches in glory by Christ Jesus' (Philippians 4:19)? Has not Your Word said, 'And you are complete in Him' (Colossians 2:10)? You are supplying all I need spiritually, physically, financially, and materially. You are taking care of my family's every need.

God wants to meet our needs.
His desire is that we be at peace
with Him and with ourselves.

My God shall supply all your need according to His riches in glory by Christ Jesus.

"As my Shepherd, You have made me to lie down in green pastures. You are leading me beside the still waters. Lord, You are restoring my soul. You are leading me in the paths of righteousness for Your Name's sake. When I do not know where to go, I listen to You and follow You. I follow the path of love, joy, peace, longsuffering, gentleness, goodness, faith, meekness, temperance, wisdom, and understanding (Galatians 5:22).

"I thank You, Lord, that You are leading me along the wonderful paths of forgiveness and tenderness toward all people. You are directing all of my ways.

"Father, I meditate on Your Word, which says, 'Trust in the LORD with all your heart, and lean not on your own understanding; in all your ways acknowledge Him, and He shall direct your paths' (Proverbs 3:5–6). I thank You that You *are* directing my paths. I acknowledge that I am just like a sheep. I do not know which way to turn many times, but I stay close to Jesus. As I read Your Word and meditate upon it, You lead me in the paths of righteousness for Your Name's sake.

"You are my Guide! You are my Shepherd, and I am following You daily. I am not afraid because everything that comes to me must pass You first. You know everything because You are in front of me, leading me all the way!

"I say with David, 'Yea, though I walk through the valley of the shadow of death, I will fear no evil.' Your Word did not say that I would stay in the valley; it said I would *go through!*

"I boldly confess, Father, that *I will fear no evil!* Why? Because You are with me, and Your rod and staff comfort me. Lord, it does not matter what I face now or in the future. If I go through the valley of the shadow of death, or have my heart broken, or go through sorrow and heartache, or face insurmountable circumstances and mountains of difficulties, *I will fear no evil!* I will not fear because there stands beside me to lead, guide, direct, and shield me, the Lord Jesus Christ.

"Lord, You are with me, and Your rod and staff comfort me. You prepare a table before me in the presence of my enemies—right in the presence of demonic powers, and even in the presence of Satan himself. You prepare a table, a banqueting table of victory, joy, and strength.

"You anoint my head with oil. My cup runs over! Surely goodness and mercy shall follow me all the days of my life, and I will dwell in the house of the Lord forever!

"Lord, this is my confession of victory! I am glad, Lord Jesus, that You are with me. I know that You will never leave me nor forsake me (see Hebrews 13:5). You are with me wherever I go; therefore, *nothing* can overcome me, because He who is in me is greater than he who is in the world (1 John 4:4). The *Father* is in me. The *Son* is in me. The *Holy Spirit* is in me. Oh Father, Son, and Holy Ghost, You are greater than any power of the enemy, any circumstances, or any problem. I am an overcomer!

"Therefore, I face life fearlessly. I confidently put these words upon my lips. When people ask me, 'Well, how is it with you?' I will boldly say, 'The Lord is my Shepherd.' I do not have a want, a care, or any anxiety.

"God made me the salt of the earth, the light of the world, and the righteousness of God. Through Jesus, I am forgiven, delivered, and healed. I am more than a conqueror. I am blessed of the Lord.

"This is my joyful declaration. I will speak it before men and they, too, shall be lifted up and blessed. As they leave my presence, people will say, 'This one is surely blessed of the Lord.'

"I praise You, Father, because I shall have whatever I say!

"God abundantly supplies all my needs!"

I WILL LIVE IN LOVE AND OBEY YOUR

COMMANDMENTS, LORD.

I will obey Your law, and I will not turn

from it to the right hand or to the left.

I will prosper wherever I go.

Reflections from
JOEL

*W*e read God's promise to Abraham, "And I will make of you a great nation, and I will bless you [with abundant increase of favors] and make your name famous and distinguished, and you will be a blessing [dispensing good to others]" (Genesis 12:2 AMP), and we often say, "All right, God! Come on; pour out Your blessings on me!"

But notice, there's a catch. We must do something; better yet, we must be something. God is implying that we will not be blessed simply so we can live lavishly or self-indulgently. We will be blessed to be a blessing. Indeed, unless we are willing to be a blessing, God will not pour out His favor and goodness in our lives. We will receive from God in the same measure we give to others.

If we'd listen more carefully, maybe we'd hear God saying, "When are you going to start being a blessing?"

CHAPTER TEN

A Declaration
of Victory
Over Fear

Jesus said that in the last days, men's hearts would fail them for fear (see Luke 21:26). Fear is a tormenting spirit (see 1 John 4:18), and far too many people live under this torment today.

Read Psalm 91 several times, and let it sink into your heart as you meditate upon it.

Make the declaration with me. Surely no day should pass without you boldly knowing this declaration so well that you can repeat it anytime and anywhere. God, by the power of His Word, will lift you to a plane of victory where every trace of fear and torment will be banished.

He who dwells in the secret place of the Most High
    Shall abide under the shadow of the Almighty.
I will say of the LORD, "He is my refuge and my fortress;
    My God, in Him I will trust."
Surely He shall deliver you from the snare of the fowler
    And from the perilous pestilence.
He shall cover you with His feathers,
    And under His wings you shall take refuge;
    His truth shall be your shield and buckler.
You shall not be afraid of the terror by night,
    Nor of the arrow that flies by day,
    Nor of the pestilence that walks in darkness,
    Nor of the destruction that lays waste at noonday.
A thousand may fall at your side,
    And ten thousand at your right hand;
    But it shall not come near you.
Only with your eyes shall you look,
    And see the reward of the wicked.
Because you have made the LORD, who is my refuge,
    Even the Most High, your dwelling place,
No evil shall befall you,
    Nor shall any plague come near your dwelling;
For He shall give His angels charge over you,
    To keep you in all your ways.

In their hands they shall bear you up,
  Lest you dash your foot against a stone.
You shall tread upon the lion and the cobra,
  The young lion and the serpent you shall trample
    underfoot.
"Because he has set his love upon Me,
    therefore I will deliver him;
  I will set him on high, because he has
    known My name.
He shall call upon Me, and I will answer him;
  I will be with him in trouble;
  I will deliver him and honor him.
With long life I will satisfy him,
  And show him My salvation."

PSALM 91

In the last three verses of this beautiful psalm, God gives us seven promises. These promises are contingent upon one fact: that we set our love upon Him. When we love Him, He will deliver us and set us on high. He will answer us when we call upon Him and be with us in trouble, and He will honor us. He will satisfy us with long life and show us His salvation.

A Personal Declaration of Victory Over Fear

"Father, I come to You with Your Word. I will not let pass from my lips that which would grieve You or harm me, but I will put Your words within my lips and confess them at Your great throne.

"I know that words can be destructive or they can be strength to those who walk uprightly. I choose to speak Your words, Father, because they are life. Your Word is eternally settled in heaven.

"You said to Joshua, the great deliverer, 'This Book of the Law shall not depart from your mouth' (Joshua 1:8).

"King David said, 'I will say of the Lord' (Psalm 91:2).

"The Word of the Lord came to the prophet Jeremiah— 'Is not My word like a fire?' says the Lord, 'and like a hammer that breaks the rock in pieces?' (Jeremiah 23:29).

"Mary, the mother of Jesus, said, 'Let it be to me according to your word' (Luke 1:38).

"Therefore, I say, let it be to me according to Your Word. I take Your Word and not only put it in my heart, but I speak it with my mouth. I confess this psalm to You. I declare that I dwell in the secret place of the Most High. I abide under the shadow of the Almighty. Lord, this is my dwelling place! It is not where I visit once in a while. I declare that I dwell in the secret place of the Most High.

"I thank You, Father, that in this wicked world in which I live, there is a secret place—a hiding place under the shadow of Your wings. Lord, that hiding place is in Your presence. Wherever I go, I can sense Your divine presence, the divine influence of Your Spirit upon my life. So I can boldly say: I dwell in the secret place of the Most High. I abide under the shadow of the Almighty.

"Oh Father, I am glad You are close to me. You said You would send another Comforter, the Holy Spirit, who will abide with me forever. My body is the temple of the Holy Spirit. I am not my own. I belong to You. I am bought with a price. Therefore, I glorify You in my body and in my spirit (see 1 Corinthians 6:19–20). You said You will walk in me and You will be my God and I will be Your child. The greater One lives within me. I dwell in the secret place of the Most High. This is my living place! In the midst of all the storms of life, all the confusion of life, all the turbulence of life, and all the troubles of life, *I am abiding under the shadow of the Almighty.*

"And what shall I say of the Lord? Shall I say He has failed me, or I do not understand the Lord, or the Lord has brought sickness and sorrow and trouble upon me? No! I will not have a negative confession and talk about my trouble, my sorrow, and all the things I do not understand. I will say what God's Word says. I boldly confess that the Lord is my refuge and my fortress. The Lord is my God; in Him will I trust.

"Surely You have delivered me from the snare of the fowler and from the noisome pestilence. You have covered me with Your feathers, and under Your wings I trust. Your truth is my shield and my buckler. This is my declaration about the Lord.

"Lord God, Your truth is what I am speaking today. I live in Your Word. I read it daily and meditate upon it. I speak it out to men, and I confess it to You. The Word of the Lord endures forever! No Word of God shall be void of power. Your Word, Father, is truth. 'All Scripture is given by inspiration of God, and is profitable for doctrine, for reproof, for correction, for instruction in righteousness, that the man of God may be complete, thoroughly equipped for every good work' (2 Timothy 3:16–17).

"Father, it is said that in the last days men's hearts will fail them because of fear, but I boldly confess that I am not afraid! I am not afraid of the powers of darkness. I am not afraid of sickness or an early death. I am not afraid of divorce! I am not afraid that my children will go astray! I am not afraid that the members of my family will never be saved! I am not afraid that You do not love me! I am not afraid of trouble, sorrow, and heartache! *I am not afraid!*

"Lord, I confess that I am bold and courageous. I am a strong person. I stand up tall and square my shoulders. I am a bold soldier of the Lord Jesus Christ! I refuse fear in my spirit, mind, and body. *I am not afraid!*

"As I read this psalm, Lord, I see what I am not afraid of. I am not afraid of the terror by night. I will not give in to intense, overpowering fear. I am not afraid of the arrow that flies by day or of the evil plots and slanders of the wicked. I am not afraid of the pestilence that walks in darkness. I do not fear any fatal epidemic or evil influence. I am not afraid of the destruction that wastes at noonday. *I am not afraid!*

"I am not afraid because God is my Father, and if He is for me, who can be against me? Lord Jesus, You are my Lord and my Savior. The Holy Spirit dwells within me, and I am surrounded by the angels of God. *I am not afraid!*

"I am going to stop and praise You with uplifted hands. I praise You, Lord. I am delivered from fear. I do not care if I feel fear or not. I am not afraid of fear. I will not entertain fear. When fear comes against my mind, I hold up the blood of Jesus and cry, 'The blood of the Lord Jesus Christ is against you!' Then those evil imaginations disappear! I realize that my God is able to deliver me out of *all* of the troubles of life!

"*I am not afraid!* I boldly declare it. I believe it in my heart and speak it with my mouth. All fear has to leave me. I have all power over all demonic forces in the Name of the Lord Jesus Christ (see Luke 10:19). I command you to flee from me according to the Word of God! Get away from all of my family! Leave now, you spirits of fear! I am not afraid.

"Father, You have not given me the spirit of fear, but the spirit of power and of love and of a sound mind (see 2 Timothy 1:7). I boldly confess that I do not have the spirit of fear, for the spirit of fear has fled from me according to Your Word, which says, 'Resist the devil and he will flee from you' (James 4:7). I boldly declare that I have the spirit of love, power, and a sound mind by Your Spirit.

"Now, the enemy would tell me that I am going to fail, my family is going to be destroyed, and tragedy is going to come. But I say boldly, 'Lord, a thousand may fall at my side and ten thousand at my right hand, but it shall not come near me. Only with my eyes shall I behold and see the reward of the wicked.' This is the Word of the eternal God, and I boldly declare that it is true! *No evil shall come near me!*

"Only with my eyes shall I see the reward of the wicked. Father, the powers of darkness aligned against me shall be rewarded with everlasting destruction from the Lord. They are eternally defeated, for Jesus spoiled principalities and powers and made a show of them openly, triumphing over them (see Colossians 2:15). He was manifested to destroy the works of the devil (see 1 John 3:8).

"Now, Father, I come to the reward of such a confession. Because I have made You my habitation, my dwelling place, and my portion, I boldly confess that no evil shall befall me, no plague or calamity shall come near my dwelling.

"Lord, this is my confession because You have given Your angels charge over me to keep me in all my ways. They will bear me up in their hands lest I dash my foot against a stone. Father, Your angels accompany me, defend me, and preserve me. Thank You, Lord, for those blessed ministering spirits. Even though I do not see them, they are busy at work every hour of the day, watching over me and my loved ones.

"I boldly confess that I tread upon the lion and the adder, and the young lion and the dragon I trample under foot. Because I have set my love upon You, Lord, You will deliver me and set me on high. You will answer me when I call upon You, and You will be with me in trouble. You will honor me, satisfy me with long life, and show me Your salvation. This is true in my life. You have answered me when I have called upon You. You are with me in trouble. You have not deserted me, but You have delivered me. You are honoring me daily with Your presence, Your power, Your mercy, and Your goodness.

"Lord, you will satisfy me with long life, and the number of my days You will fulfill (see Exodus 23:26). I will not die an early death. Sickness will not take my life prematurely. I thank You, Father, that You are all powerful.

"Father, I confidently rejoice in You because You are the preserver of my life. You are the strength of my life. You are the God of this universe, and You are my very own Father! I do not fear or fret! I am full of love, joy, peace, and power.

"Father, I will share the Good News with those around me. I will not have an evil report, but I will have a good report. No words shall pass my lips except that which pertains to Your Word. This is my confession. I praise You, Father, because you are watching over Your Word to see that it is fulfilled in my life (see Jeremiah 1:12).

"I have victory over fear!"

GOD, BY THE POWER OF HIS WORD,

will lift you to a plane of victory where

every trace of fear and torment will be banished.

Reflections from
JOEL

King David said, "You prepare a table before me in the presence of my enemies; You anoint my head with oil; my cup runs over" (Psalm 23:5).

How would you feel if you prepared a delicious dinner and spread the food out on the table, but your children come in, refuse to sit at the table, and instead crawl under the table and wait for some scraps or crumbs to fall? For whatever reason, they don't feel good enough to sit at the table and enjoy the food as well as your company.

Friend, do you want to make your heavenly Father happy? Then start stepping up to the dinner table and enjoying His blessings. You don't have to live in guilt and condemnation any longer; you don't have to go through life full of fear and worry. The price has been paid. Come into the banquet hall and take your rightful place as His child.

CHAPTER ELEVEN

A Declaration

of

What Jesus
Is *to* Me

The following declaration will change what you believe about yourself. Take time to meditate on Psalm 27. As you read and confess it aloud day after day, you will come to know that the Lord is your light and salvation. You will know that you have nothing to fear because He is the strength of your life.

> *The Lord is my light and my salvation;*
> *Whom shall I fear?*
> *The Lord is the strength of my life;*
> *Of whom shall I be afraid?*

When the wicked came against me
  To eat up my flesh,
  My enemies and foes,
  They stumbled and fell.
Though an army may encamp against me,
  My heart shall not fear;
  Though war may rise against me,
  In this I will be confident.
One thing I have desired of the LORD,
  That will I seek:
  That I may dwell in the house of the LORD
  All the days of my life,
  To behold the beauty of the LORD,
  And to inquire in His temple.
For in the time of trouble
  He shall hide me in His pavilion;
  In the secret place of His tabernacle
  He shall hide me;
  He shall set me high upon a rock.
And now my head shall be lifted up above my
          enemies all around me;
  Therefore I will offer sacrifices of joy
          in His tabernacle;
  I will sing, yes, I will sing praises to the LORD.

PSALM 27:1–6

A Personal Confession of What Jesus Is to Me

"Father, I come to Your throne, rejoicing that I am washed in the blood of the Lamb of God. I rejoice that I am a new creature in Christ Jesus and that You are my Father and I am Your child.

"Lord, as I approach Your great and wonderful throne, I confess Your Word and have whatever I say. As I approach Your throne, confessing Psalm 27, it will not be written words only, but it shall become living words to me because I claim it as my own.

"You said, in Deuteronomy 11:24, 'Every place on which the sole of your foot treads shall be yours.' Today I put the soles of my feet as if they were on Psalm 27, and I claim that land as my own. Father, I boldly confess Your Word and declare that these great truths are mine.

"I say with King David, Lord, You are my light and my salvation; whom shall I fear? Lord, You are the strength of my life; of whom shall I be afraid? Oh my Father, I praise You because the Lord Jesus is the light of the world. Jesus said to me, 'You are the light of the world' (Matthew 5:14). I thank You, Lord Jesus, that You are my light! I will not walk in darkness because I know the Light of life. I will not be afraid of the darkness of this generation. I thank You, O Lord, that You are my light.

"Jesus, You live in me, and You are my salvation. Salvation is forgiveness, healing, deliverance, wholeness, health, peace, and rest. Jesus, You are my salvation. You are all I will ever need to be free from the power of the enemy. I flee unto the rock that is higher than I am. You are that rock. In You are hidden all the treasures of the wisdom and knowledge of God (see Colossians 2:3). Lord Jesus, I am complete in You.

"You are my light and my salvation. You are the strength of my life. You live on the inside of me, and Your strength is my strength. Lord God, I can boldly say that I have light, health, and strength. I have the Lord Jesus Christ!

"I am in Christ, and Christ is in me! Oh Father, I praise You for Your Son. Lord Jesus, You said if any man serve You, him will Your Father honor. Father, You have honored me with life, strength, and salvation both day and night. I am so glad that I walk in the blessings of God.

"Lord God, You are my Father. Jesus, You are my Lord. The Holy Spirit is my comforter, helper, and strengthener. Therefore, I am not afraid of anyone or anything. *I am not afraid!* I fear not! I am not dismayed because the Lord my God is with me wherever I go. When the wicked, even my enemies and my foes, come upon me, they stumble and fall. This is my confession. When demonic powers come against me mentally, spiritually, physically, emotionally, and maritally, they stumble and fall!

"I am covered by the blood of the Lord Jesus Christ, and no power of darkness can cross that hedge. They must stumble and fall. The blood of the Lord Jesus Christ is over me, and the angel of the Lord encamps round about me. Though an army encamp against me, my heart will not fear. Goodness and mercy follow me, and the Lord goes before me. Underneath me are Your everlasting arms.

"I desire one thing, Lord, and this will I seek after—that I may dwell in the house of the Lord all the days of my life, to behold the beauty of the Lord and to inquire in Your holy temple. Lord, I have confidence in You because I desire, more than anything else in the world, to have a relationship with You, to behold Your beauty, and to live in Your presence.

"I know that we all will have trouble, but in the time of trouble, Father, You hide me in Your pavilion. In the secret of Your tabernacle, You hide me and set me upon a rock. That rock is the Lord Jesus Christ, and He is high above all of my enemies where they cannot reach me. So I say with the psalmist that my head is now lifted up above my enemies round about me. Oh yes, I am lifted up!

The Lord is my light and my salvation;
Whom shall I fear?

"I am more than a conqueror through the Lord Jesus Christ. I am set upon the rock, and I will not be shaken. I will not be defeated, for greater is He that is in me than he that is in the world. Therefore, I say with King David, I will offer in Your tabernacle sacrifices of joy. I will sing, yes, I will sing praises unto the Lord. I am not going to moan and groan and complain. I offer sacrifices of joy and sing praises unto the Lord. Blessed be the Name of the Lord!

"I rejoice because Christ Jesus is my victory! He is my great Conqueror and He lives within me. I run through a troop and leap over a wall by the Name of the Lord, my God. I have overcome by the power of His Name.

"Father, this is my declaration as I face life with all of its problems, with all of its heartaches, with all the things that would engulf me with despair. I will not look at my circumstances. I will not dwell upon my situation, Lord, but I will say boldly and confidently these things about You. I will rejoice that these truths are actually becoming a part of my life. I believe them within my heart. I speak them with my mouth, and they are indeed made mine daily because the Bible says I shall have whatever I say.

"I rejoice that Psalm 27 is mine. I will meditate upon it, confess it, talk about it, and rejoice that it is mine.

Jesus is my light and my salvation!"

Reflections from
JOEL

To live your best life now requires that you believe you are a victor and not a victim. When you go through disappointments in life—and we all do—or when you face a setback and it looks as though one of your dreams has died, keep believing. When it looks dark and dreary and you don't see any way out, remind yourself that your heavenly Father created the whole universe. He is in control of your life, guiding and directing your steps. His plans for you are good and not evil. Don't make the mistake of sitting around feeling sorry for yourself. No, put on a fresh new attitude. Take what God has given you and make the most of it.

You know the truth; it's time to allow that truth to set you free. "But thanks be to God, who gives us the victory through our Lord Jesus Christ" (1 Corinthians 15:57).

CHAPTER TWELVE

Keep What God Gives

The Bible says, "Blessed is every one who fears the LORD, who walks in His ways. When you eat the labor of your hands, you shall be happy, and it shall be well with you. Your wife shall be like a fruitful vine in the very heart of your house, your children like olive plants all around your table. Behold, thus shall the man be blessed who fears the LORD" (Psalm 128:1–4).

God wants us to be a blessed people. As a good Father, He wants to give us good things to enjoy in this life. Now I realize that many of us have already received the good things that God has given.

He has given us health.

He has given us strength.

He has given us financial blessings.

He has given us healing—mental, emotional, and physical.

He has blessed us with wonderful families, and many other things that we rejoice in.

Did you know, however, that there is an enemy who wants to steal and destroy all that God has given you? Perhaps you have already lost or are in danger of losing some of the blessings of God. My desire is to help you.

THREE THINGS SATAN WANTS TO DO

The Bible teaches us that Satan is the god of this world (2 Corinthians 4:4). He once was a beautiful angel in heaven, but he became lifted up in pride and rebelled against God. He was thrown out of heaven and down to the earth with many other angels who rebelled with him (Ezekiel 28:11–19). These fallen angels became evil spirits that are organized under Satan's command (Ephesians 6:10–12).

Satan is the enemy of the Church, and he works with great fury to destroy anyone who would be deceived by him. Thank God we know the truth about him! We have been delivered from Satan's power and kingdom because Jesus defeated him for us on the cross. Now, we have power over all the power of the enemy, and nothing shall by any means hurt us (Luke 10:18–19). Satan has absolutely no legal or spiritual right or authority in your life. However, that does not stop him from trying his best to deceive and defeat you.

The following three passages of Scripture describe three things that Satan is intent on doing to you if you remain ignorant of his devices.

- *"When an unclean spirit goes out of a man, he goes through dry places, seeking rest, and finds none. Then he says, 'I will return to my house from which I came.' And when he comes, he finds it empty, swept, and put in order. Then he goes and takes with him seven other spirits more wicked than himself, and they enter and dwell there; and the last state of that man is worse than the first"* (Matthew 12:43–45).
- *"The thief does not come except to steal, and to kill, and to destroy. I have come that they may have life, and that they may have it more abundantly"* (John 10:10).
- *"Be sober, be vigilant; because your adversary the devil walks about like a roaring lion, seeking whom he may devour"* (1 Peter 5:8).

You will notice these scriptures tell us three things that Satan is determined to do:

1. Satan will try to return.
2. He will try to steal, kill, and destroy.
3. He will try to devour.

This chapter is to help you know how to keep the enemy from accomplishing his goal. I believe it is possible to stand fast as more than a conqueror. God is going to help you as you read and meditate upon the truths written in this book. My deepest desire is to inform God's people of the precious grace, mercy, and knowledge of God. You need to know how to rise up with a personal knowledge of who you are in Christ and not have to depend on anyone else. You can stand in the thick of the battle unwavering and unfaltering, with the Name of Jesus Christ, and send the enemy fleeing in terror from you!

It is important that you know how to keep the blessings that God has given you, whether they are wonderful health, financial prosperity, emotional stability, mental peace, or marital blessings.

Satan's Counterattack

I want you to know that you will not enjoy the blessings of God without being contested by your enemy. He will leave you alone for a while, then he will make a counterattack and surprise and alarm you. Many people lose what God has given them when Satan makes his counterattack. Many go back into poverty, emotional instability, and mental torment. They say, "I thought God had visited me with His blessings. It looks as though I have lost it all."

You need to know how to keep what God has given you.

Did you know that you can lose your blessings by ignorance as well as sin? Hosea 4:6 states, "My people are destroyed for lack of knowledge." People need more than inspiration; they need information. Let's look at the Word of God and get Bible information that will help us.

In all three texts quoted at the beginning of this chapter, we have a revelation of three things the devil is determined to do. In Matthew 12:43, Jesus revealed that it is the devil's stated purpose to come back against you. He wants to reenter your life in some phase. He said, "I will return to my house."

He is too ignorant to know that your body is the temple of God. He still thinks it is his house. We once belonged to him, but now we belong to God (Ephesians 2:2–5). When we were dead in trespasses, God made us alive together with Christ. First Corinthians 6:19–20 states: "Or do you not know that your body is the temple of the Holy Spirit who is in you, whom you have from God, and you are not your own? For you were bought at a price; therefore glorify God in your body and in your spirit, which are God's."

Can you imagine some demon talking with other demons about your precious body and calling it, "his house"? Nevertheless, he said, "I will return."

Friend, the devil is determined to return and try to take control of your life mentally, physically, financially, emotionally, and every other way. He is going to try to come back into your life in some area.

In John 10:10, it says that he is going to try to steal and to kill and to destroy. These are revelation scriptures that tell you clearly the thoughts of your enemy. Satan says, "I will steal what God has given you. I will kill your dreams and desires. I will destroy

You can stand in the thick of the battle unwavering and unfaltering, with the Name of Jesus Christ, and send the enemy fleeing in terror from you!

your business and destroy your peace and destroy your happiness." He is an evil prince with demon forces under his command, and he sends them forth to steal, kill, and destroy. Some people think that if they just stick their head in the sand and ignore him, he will go away. No, he won't. He will come at you from every side. Just ignoring the devil does not send him away. He's determined to steal everything he can from you. He is out to destroy you.

Don't Blame God!

As a pastor, I have counseled many brokenhearted people in tragic situations. Some of them have asked me, "Why has God done this to me?" They are angry and bitter with God.

Wouldn't it be refreshing for someone to come and say, "Why has Satan done this to me? I'll never give in to him!"

Far too often people blame God for what the devil does, especially when it comes to their health. The enemy is determined to steal our health and replace it with misery! He has said, "I will return to my house. I will steal, I will kill, and I will destroy."

Be sober! Be vigilant! Be on your toes!
Be keen! Don't get apathetic or careless!
Don't let your guard down!

First Peter 5:8 reads: "Be sober, be vigilant; because your adversary the devil walks about like a roaring lion, seeking whom he may devour." Be sober! Be vigilant! Be on your toes! Be keen! Don't get apathetic or careless! Don't let your guard down!

Isn't it a tragedy that while the powers of darkness are so vigilant, so constant, so alert, and so active that some of God's people are not alert and active, but would rather sit down and say, "Well, I don't think we should take the Word of God literally. Some of it just doesn't make sense to me. I can't expect God to work today as He did in the Bible times." While our adversary walks about as a roaring lion, seeking whom he may devour, they sit on their hands passively and let the powers of darkness do whatever they want!

Never has the kingdom of darkness been more active than today. At every level of society we are seeing an unprecedented attack on biblical values and standards, and the result is the erosion and breakdown of the fabric that God meant to hold our lives together. If there was ever a day when we needed truth and to stand for truth, it is today!

Satan's purpose is to take from you what God has given you.

Let's see what God tells us to do.

Hold Fast That Which You Already Have!

Jesus said in Revelation 2:25, "But hold fast what you have till I come."

Some people think if God gave it to them, it is forever theirs. Well, it is, but somebody is going to try to steal it. The devil will try to take it from you. God says, "Hold fast what you already have!" Stand your ground! Resist the devil!

The Bible reveals your rights and privileges in Christ. As you feed on the Word of God, you will know how to keep what God has given you.

Some people say, "Well, I thought God healed me, but here I am feeling all the symptoms again. And I thought God gave me His blessing on my business, but now it's failing. I thought I was blessed!"

The reason God tells you to hold fast is because there is a force that is going to seek to pull your blessings away from you. You are not going to keep your healing, you are not going to keep your blessings, and you are not going to keep all the good things of God if you get passive and let the devil slip up and take them away from you. The Bible says, "But hold fast what you have till I come!"

I remember when our house was paid off, what a joyous day it was! Now, what if I came home one day and some burly fellow was sitting in my debt-free house and said to me, "My family and I decided this is our new house." Would I just say, "Well, I thought it was mine, but come on, Dodie; come on, children. We have to get out"? My wife would say, "No, this is my house!" And I would fight him "tooth and toenail!" I am not going to work and pray and believe God to pay for my house just to have anyone, big or little, come in and take what is rightfully and legally mine!

In a similar manner, many Christians are not fighting for what is rightfully theirs. Satan comes around to steal everything, and they just roll over and act as though it's his. You have a legal document—the Bible. Read it to the devil and command him in Jesus' Name to go!

This reminds me of our German shepherd, Scooter. I used to ride a bicycle around our neighborhood, and he would trot along beside me. I was so proud of that dog. Scooter was so big and strong and healthy looking that he could "whip" a lion. He would run like a deer, and I bragged on my dog everywhere I went.

One day I was riding along and a little tiny dog just about five inches tall came running out at Scooter. Its legs were hardly bigger than matchsticks. As I watched him bark, I thought, *Scooter is going to eat him up with one bite. Watch out, little dog!* But that dog ran toward my big fine dog, yapping and barking up a storm, and Scooter just turned over on his back, put up all four feet, and gave up!

I was so shocked. Scooter could have put one paw on that little dog and that would have ended it! But he just rolled over and said, "I give up." I don't know what that little dog said in dog talk, but he was convincing!

Some believers act just like my dog Scooter in the face of a spiritual attack. A voice starts yapping and telling them, "You're not going to get well. You have all the symptoms again. You are going to go broke. You are going to lose this and lose that. You will never be free of your addiction." They just roll over, tremble in fear, and throw in the towel.

No! Stand up on your feet! Use the Name of Jesus! Hold fast that which you already have! Don't give the enemy one thing God has given you. It does not belong to him. You have a legal document. It is written in the Word of God. This legal document says abundant life is yours.

Hold Fast Your Confession

What else does God tell us to do? Hebrews 4:14 says, "Let us hold fast our confession." Don't change your confession. Don't change your words. Don't begin to agree with what the enemy tells you. Friend, if you begin to change what you say, you will lose it.

How are you to hold on to what God has given you? Renew your mind every day in the Word of God. Romans 12:2 states, "And do not be conformed to this world, but be transformed by the renewing of your mind, that you may prove what is that good and acceptable and perfect will of God."

Let God's Word live big in you.

Colossians 3:16 states: "Let the word [spoken by] Christ (the Messiah) have its home [in your hearts and minds] and dwell in you in [all its] richness" (AMP). Live in the Word. Learn it until, as Jesus did in Matthew 4, you can say, "It is written," and drive away the devil every time he attacks you.

Renew your mind in the Word of God. *Think the thoughts of God,* your heavenly Father.

God tells you to hold fast to what you already have. Hold fast to your confession. Don't ever change what you are saying. Say what God says about you. It does not matter if every symptom of financial distress, emotional upset, or physical disease comes. Hold fast to your confession.

When the enemy attacks you, what are you going to do? Will you roll over like my dog Scooter? Will you just accept defeat? Is that what you are going to do? Or are you going to act like the mighty sons and daughters of God? When the going gets tough, the tough get going!

You need to know the Bible yourself. You need to find out who you are in Christ. You need to know how to stand your ground! You need to do it yourself!

I put notes all over my house that remind me of God's promises. I boldly declare my place in Christ.

You need to know four things:

1. You need to know who Christ is.
2. You need to know what Christ has done for you.
3. You need to know who you are in Christ.
4. You need to know what you can do in the power of the Name of Jesus.

If you remain ignorant and passive, if you refuse to take biblical teachings seriously, I guarantee that when the devil comes, you will not be ready for him. You will be no match for him! Why? Because you have discounted the very thing that will set you free!

Boldly make this confession:

> *I know who I am in Christ!*
> *I know what I can do in Christ!*
> *I bear the Name of Jesus!*
> *I am washed by the blood of Jesus!*
> *I am in the family of God!*
> *I have the life of God in me!*
> *I am filled with the Spirit of God!*
> *I am in the kingdom of God!*
> *I resist the devil and he flees from me!*

In your spiritual life, I want you to stand up tall. Do not murmur as the Israelites, for many of them were destroyed (Deuteronomy 2:26–28). There is always something destroyed when you murmur. Quit murmuring! Quit complaining! Quit being weak. Learn who you are in God. "If you can believe, all things are possible to him who believes" (Mark 9:23).

Your greatest dream, your highest aspirations can come true. You may be thinking, *You are talking about holding on to it when you get it, but I don't even have it yet!* Yes, you do! All the blessings of God are already yours. Jesus already died and rose again to give you all of God's blessings.

Salvation and healing have already been provided in the redemptive work of the cross. All you need is to find the scriptures that pertain to your situation and believe them. You could have been free a long time ago if only you had known about it and believed God for it!

Speak what God says about you. Make these declarations about yourself:

- *I am of God (1 John 4:4).*
- *I have overcome the evil one (1 John 4:4).*
- *Greater is He that is in me, than he that is in the world (1 John 4:4).*
- *Christ has redeemed me from the curse of the law (Galatians 3:13).*
- *I am living in the blessings of Abraham (Galatians 3:14).*
- *I am blessed in the city. I am blessed in the field (Deuteronomy 28:3).*
- *I am blessed when I go out. I am blessed when I come in (Deuteronomy 28:6).*
- *I know who I am in Christ. I bear the Name of Jesus. Satan will not steal one thing that God has given me (John 10:10).*

- *I am strong in the Lord and the power of His might (Ephesians 6:10).*
- *I have on the whole armor of God (Ephesians 6:11).*
- *I am able to stand against all the wiles and all the strategies of the enemy (Ephesians 6:11).*
- *I stand my ground. Having done all, I stand (Ephesians 6:13).*
- *I am more than a conqueror (Romans 8:37).*
- *I will not be ashamed of Jesus or His Word (Romans 1:16).*
- *I will stand tall as a child of God!*
- *I will bear the Name that is above every name, the Name of Jesus (Philippians 2:9–10).*
- *I will drive the enemy from the field of battle (James 4:7).*
- *Healing is mine (1 Peter 2:24).*
- *Wholeness is mine (3 John 2).*
- *Prosperity is mine (Deuteronomy 28:8, 12).*
- *The blessing of God is mine (Galatians 3:14).*
- *All my needs have been supplied. I will begin to act like it (Philippians 4:19).*
- *God's blessings are mine! The devil will not rob me.*
- *I will keep what God has given me (Revelation 2:25).*

If you remain ignorant and passive, if you refuse to take biblical teachings seriously, I guarantee that when the devil comes, you will not be ready for him.

MAKE THIS YOUR PRAYER

"Dear Father, I come boldly to Your throne to claim my benefits in the kingdom of God. I have an inheritance that You have given me, and I claim it in the high court of heaven.

"Thank You that You so loved me that You gave Your only Son that I might have eternal life. I have the assurance of that eternal life because the Holy Spirit within me bears witness in my heart that I am Your child.

"Thank You that I have received the promise of the Holy Spirit, who gives me continuing power to live a godly life and to be a witness of the Lord Jesus Christ.

"I am healed, and I have been given perfect health, for by Jesus' stripes I was healed and I am healed now.

"I have authority over Satan and nothing shall by any means hurt me because greater is He that is in me than he that is in the world. I submit myself to God, and as I resist the devil, he must flee!

"Thank You, Father, that Your will gives me prosperity of body and soul. My every need is met according to Your riches in glory by Christ Jesus. As I give, men give to me. As I seek first Your kingdom and Your righteousness, all things are added to me.

"According to Your will, I am the righteousness of God in Christ. I will not cower under condemnation from the enemy. I will walk in the Spirit, for Christ Jesus has been made to me righteousness.

"Father, You have not given me a spirit of fear, but of power and of love and of a sound mind. God's perfect love in me and for me casts out all fear in my life. I am free. And whom the Son sets free is free indeed!

"Your Word gives me the weapons of my warfare, which include the gifts of the Holy Spirit. I will desire and earnestly cultivate these gifts of the Spirit that I might edify and build up the body of Christ.

"Thank You, Father, that You have heard my prayer, for I ask in Jesus' Name. You have said that if I ask anything in His Name that You will do it. I receive the benefits of Your will this day with joy and thanksgiving, giving glory to God.

"In Jesus' Name. Amen."

Reflections from
JOEL